YOUTH CONSIDERS
DOUBT
AND
FRUSTRATION

YOUTH FORUM SERIES

Titles in Print

YOUTH FORUM SERIES

Youth Considers
DOUBT
AND
FRUSTRATION

by

Paul L. Holmer

THOMAS NELSON & SONS

London   CAMDEN, N.J.   *Toronto*

Library of Congress Catalog Card Number: 65-22018

design by Harold Leach

Printed in the United States of America

Foreword

Written in the context of the Christian faith, this book is one in a series published by Thomas Nelson & Sons in collaboration with Church Youth Research.

The research agency, which serves as editor of this series, is known through *What Youth Are Thinking* (Smedsrud, 1961) and *Profiles of Church Youth* (Strommen, 1963). The Director, Dr. Merton Strommen, is known also for his work as Director of Research (1965-67) with Religious Education Association, an inter-faith agency serving all church groups.

The purpose of the series is to use points of established need to bring about meaningful contact between the GOSPEL of God in Jesus Christ and YOUNG PEOPLE. Underlying the total effort is a concern that youth throughout the English-speaking world can be helped to see that the Gospel of Christ is the core of life itself in all its realities.

Unique to this publication effort is the use that is made of research findings. These describe the specific need to which each book is addressed as well as the youth most concerned about this need. Thus a writer is helped to speak more directly to the actual conflicts, values, and beliefs of an important segment of youth.

The significance of this series is enhanced by the scholarship and pastoral concern of the authors. Their grasp of the fields in which each writes enables them to speak with authority, establishing the series as a basic reference in the area of youth work.

Preface

These pages are written for all, young or old, who have learned to doubt. Perhaps that does not omit even you; for doubting seems to be quite common these days, certainly about many religious and moral concerns. Besides, doubting, it must be remembered, is actually learned just as believing surely is. Recently it has appeared that the young people among us are learning the doubts of their elders, as well as most of their other attitudes and concerns, much earlier than previous generations did.

Years ago, doubting such serious matters as religion and morals was a sign of long turmoil and great gravity of spirit. Only an arduous and long life, seasoned with a stiff dose of cynicism or despair, or with the discovery of strange and new truths, could possibly cause men to doubt. Clearly enough, things have changed. Once people began by believing and doubted, if at all, only much later; now they begin by doubting. Attitudes of disbelief, skepticism, and uncertainty now seem to be most widespread among high-school and college students.

All kinds of people have thought about this state of affairs. To some it looks as though we are in an age of doubt, created by more mature sciences and critical scrutiny, quite different than in earlier days of mythology and superstition. Others have seen the doubt of the age as a distressing loss of capacity to live and to love with abandon and confidence, even a severing of our roots with things precious and old. On the other hand, some very learned religious men, usually the theologians, have exercised their wit and concern for these new unbelievers. Various arguments and theologies have been and are being designed, ostensibly to meet the "new age," the "scientific temper," and whatever else is thought to be responsible for the situation.

However, this brief book does not attempt any such new theology. It does not, therefore, try to meet the doubts by discovering some unquestionable truths that cannot be doubted.

Neither does it propose some new way of putting matters that will make believing easier. Instead, these pages are addressed to the reader, young or old, in the conviction that the seat of the difficulty is not in the teachings but in the manner and use of them—in short, the "how" of understanding them. Therefore, the author is quite content to leave the teachings alone, neither desiring to substitute new ones for the old nor seeking to reinterpret them in ways more congenial or more applicable to present circumstances.

All kinds of things can be said about these issues, but it will be quite enough to hope that the reader will understand how doubting comes about, its several varieties, its power over us, and even how to resolve and to relieve it. The assumption that the Bible and other teachings are directly the cause of the doubt will certainly be questioned. On the other hand, the related notion that a new theology or a new interpretation of Scripture is all that is necessary will also be challenged.

These pages are written in the conviction that we doubt only in order to know and to believe in a better way. St. Augustine concluded that we fight wars for the sake of peace, rather than endure peace to prepare for war. So, too, it will be contended here that a mature and just belief is more appropriate to our desire and to the state of affairs than is doubt. It goes without lengthy saying that such belief is not simply credulity nor is it the same as being naive. Some doubting is surely the sign that credulity is at an end, but often doubting is not healthy and a means to a nobler end. There are cases that are more serious, where doubts bring deep dismay and sustain a corrosive unhappiness. We can only dare the conviction that men are made for joy and peace. It is too high a price to pay, namely, to revert to credulous belief, in the attempt to gain peace and solace, especially when the Christian way allows something else. For these pages do suggest another path, one of mature confidence and trust, joy yet tough-mindedness, by which faith can be combined with common human honesty.

Paul L. Holmer
Yale University
New Haven, Conn.

Contents

On Doubting

Perhaps everyone reading these pages has had serious doubts about very important matters. One time I visited a young man who was imprisoned, it turned out, on false charges. He spoke very eloquently about the injustice and unfairness of his imprisonment, but then he said that the most serious matter by far was that now he doubted everybody. No one was worth believing in any more—neither judges nor parents, neither friends nor clergy, for none of them had inquired into the charges with appropriate care.

This young person had a point. His own history had been very spotty indeed. He had taken cars without permission, he had skipped school repeatedly, he had broken rules without any apparent regard for the consequences. So, when one more charge was made against him, everyone seemed to lose patience. Parents and clergy, friends, and even the judge believed that he was guilty, and he was imprisoned. All of them "believed" something to be true about him. Apparently they "believed" that he had no character and therefore that he must be guilty in this particular case. The boy, on the contrary, asserted that he was not guilty. Very slowly the facts became evident and the boy was released, for it was determined that he had not committed that crime after all.

The unfortunate consequence was, however, the doubt born in this young person's life. When he said that he doubted everybody, that meant that he took no one at his word, that he believed most people to be liars and deceivers, that he trusted no one any more for help, that he lost the capacity to confide, to console, and to be consoled. Scarcely anyone who knew him failed to remark upon the change that came over him; for after his unwarranted punishment he seemed morose, defiant, suspicious, and almost hopeless.

This is, of course, only one kind of doubting, and perhaps it is not the most common. Still, there are lots of instances very close to it. With the coming of maturity, many young people seem to doubt that marriage is as glorious as pompous weddings and romantic talk has made it appear. They get a jaundiced and bored air about, almost as if they were tired of it before they had even tried it. So, too, high school and college, teachers and education—all of which are invariably praised and recommended as the cure for youthful ills—are often seen to be terribly human and even ordinary. The result is frequently a cynical disbelief, a kind of scornful tolerance, and an apathetic despair about the entire business of learning. And the lofty ambitions that are dangled before young people, namely, to be a professional, to be well educated, to be cultured, to be always moral, to be a good wife or husband, to be a parent, to be law abiding— these and more—sometimes become sickeningly familiar. In short, many of us plainly get fed up with all the lofty talk and the big programs—marriage, morals, career, and parenthood.

Much of this kind of doubting develops when we learn the truth about people and places. The close inspection that marriage often gets from romantic adolescents causes some of them to see that there is a lot there that is not in the popular literature and beliefs about married life. Babies, debts, ill-tempered fathers, slovenly mothers, supermarket food, and the only occasional common joys—these are quite enough to tarnish the shiny talk. Sometimes persons are spoken of as being "realists" when they know and admit the facts to be as they are. It appears that much of the doubting of our idealistic institutions and practices, such as those associated with marriage, home, and mother, is fired up by exposure to the facts. So the word gets around that believing in patriotism, in government, in learning, in the family and marriage, and in other matters too, including religion, is a feature of underexposed and naive people.

Some of this might well be the case. For example, being patriotic is another and important way to be highly idealistic. By idealistic, here, I mean only that one is asked to look at the goals, the aims, the purposes. These are the "ideals," the controlling ideas for which we are asked to have concern and enthusiasm. When one hears talk about America as the land of opportunity for all, the land of the free, and the country of justice and fair play, we are certainly being urged to have affection, to work for its survival and prosperity, and to care for America in a thousand ways. Certainly people who "believe" in America and who are patriotic are also people who are idealistic. Something like this is the case with people who "believe" in marriage or in education or in the rule of law. When we give our approval to the ideals that can be served, and when we remember them, we become enthusiastic and stimulated, anxious perhaps to get started ourselves in such directions as are suggested.

In some such way it must be that most of us have wanted to be Americans with real vengeance! Equality for everybody—how noble that sounds—for tired immigrants, deprived blacks, and dirty whites. Hardly anyone can fail to rise to almost lyrical delight over the prospects of a new nation conceived in liberty with the thought that justice will be for all. But then we suddenly discover the facts. We learn to our chagrin that Italian immigrants in New York do not want European Jews moving into their neighborhoods, that respectable whites want Negroes to stay in their place, that the honorable English of New England care little for the Irish, and that a quota system for immigration is one way to keep America the way most people seem to want it. All of a sudden those ideals, those songs and sentiments, seem terribly hollow and cheap. Instead of remaining believers in the American ideals and dream, we easily succumb to what we think is the realist's view. The facts are assumed to be responsible for our doubt and disbelief.

Again, let it be urged that something like this seems to occur on several big matters. I have mentioned marriage and family as one distinctive arena where the disbelief crops up quite readily. Patriotism and love for one's country is another; education is perhaps another. In these cases, being idealistic seems to be almost a matter of childishness. The impression arises that it is part of the silliness of children, their readiness to believe almost anything they are told. Or it is sometimes thought to be a work of older people who do not really believe it themselves but who say these things in order to dress up the ugly facts to get others to do what they want them to do.

Most of these things would not be worth saying in this brief book if it were not the case that the Christian religion comes in for the same sort of doubting too. For, whatever else it does, the religion of the churches gets all tangled up with these other idealistic endeavors. It is quite common to find that young people especially will come to disbelieve or to doubt religion along with one or more of the disbeliefs previously noted. Again the facts seem to cause the negative response. For with exposure to the ministers and the priests, with a clearer grasp of the church's role or lack of it, and with a comparison of new scientific teachings about the world to those often associated with religious groups, a kind of doubt about religion seems not only appropriate but long overdue.

Besides this there are many competing religious views. Wherever one becomes even a little at home to the big differences in belief and practice, it is tempting to say that none of them can really matter too much. Therefore, we must admit that being sophisticated is now an accomplishment for many people. In earlier times, even for those now middle-aged, there were not as many opportunities to be exposed to the diversity of convictions and beliefs that are around us. What some learned slowly and only with years and much travel is now learned very quickly.

Popular learning, television, libraries, wide and chance acquaintance have now made sophistication also relatively easy. With this early exposure has come what every reader of this page will readily identify in himself: namely, the capacity to doubt the beliefs he was taught in his childhood.

There is no easy resolution of these matters. But in what follows, a closer examination of religious doubt will be attempted. This will be done not to provide some ready-made answers to the many questions and certainly not to supply beliefs where there are only doubts. Rather it will be assumed that every reader has powers of his own by which he can make up his mind. All that I will try to do is to make the reader see what is involved so that nothing important is being missed. Thus far, I have noted that our disbeliefs have some similarities; now, I would like to stress the differences between our doubts.

2.   INNOCENT AND NON-INNOCENT BELIEVING

There is, of course, a kind of innocent believing. All kinds of people believe all kinds of things simply because they are told. We can properly speak of children as being innocent. They are innocent in several senses. For one, they are innocent morally because they do not know that there is both good and evil. When someone does not know that there are alternative possibilities, the right way and the wrong way, he is morally innocent. Remember that our courts do not hold a person responsible for wrong-doing if he is either a child (and hence morally innocent) or if he is otherwise incapable of distinguishing right from wrong.

The story of Adam and Eve tells us that they were morally innocent before they ate of the fruit of the tree of knowledge. That strange tree imparted knowledge of good and evil. Once they had eaten of it, they were aware that they were naked, and all kinds of moral and immoral considerations suddenly destroyed their innocence. Little children who are innocent and ignorant of what can be involved in their nakedness often delight in removing their clothes and prancing about. But an adult, unless he is preverse or blasé, is troubled by all kinds of considerations, and he will certainly never freely cavort as does the child. The sign of losing one's innocence in the moral sense is not simply the loss of sexual innocence. It is, instead, the fact that there is an alternative, another possibility, something to allure and attract one. In short, there is no moral innocence whenever there is a temptation to have it otherwise. Temptation is the name for the options, the good and the evil always involved.

But this is said only to make clear another sense of innocence. People are also innocent in an intellectual sense. Most of us have been taught to believe. We have not only been taught the beliefs, but we have also been taught all kinds of behavior that go with the beliefs. We have been taught to be obedient, to comply, to give in, to conform. These are not necessarily bad. Amid all of these we are taught to believe, usually in an innocent way. We do not know that there are alternatives. Our intellectual innocence here is the name for our ignorance of alternative views and beliefs. Our moral innocence is a name for our ignorance of alternative possible ways to behave. Of course, these two ways to describe our innocence overlap somewhat.

For the moment, it might be well to dwell on believing in this manner. When we are young we are taught to love and to admire our country. Perhaps we believe that it is the best country in the whole world—the strongest, most beautiful, and richest. But we probably believe this in a state of innocence. We believe, in all likelihood, simply because we are told. We are likely to continue to believe this because our country is the only one we know about—we are innocent of any knowledge of other countries. Such patriotism as this perhaps does not long persist, however. It comes as something of a shock to learn that other countries have larger armies, longer histories, perhaps more encompassing and homogeneous cultures.

The real test of patriotism comes when one learns the greatness of other nations, not simply their weaknesses. A good case in point is the sort of loose talk our nation has permitted about communist nations. For a long while now there have been all kinds of pressures to make it very clear how bad the communist nations really are. And so we have learned that their economies do not equal ours, that their governments are dictatorial and repressive, and that all kinds of things are wrong with them. Lately and certainly not too soon we have seen their art, their music, their popular culture, and many people have come to know citizens of the communist nations. It is not true that this means that everyone thereafter will become a Communist, but it is true that Americans will become less innocent about other nations and their political needs.

One remains innocent of other nations if he knows only their weaknesses and their problems. And this is what propaganda does for any people; namely, maintain the case one is dedicated to by carefully screening the facts and selecting the themes for popular attention. We can only hope that Americans and Western Europeans, on one side, and Communists of whatever nation, on the other, will oblige their own citizenry by providing a full and an objective account of the lives and histories of other nations, as well as their own. For a loyalty or a patriotism that survives only in innocence of all of the facts remains childish and immature. It is a strange and almost perverse patriotism that can last only if some of the facts are known. The best kind of citizen is the responsible sort that, even when the facts and the problems are known, will nonetheless persist in loyalty and affection. A citizen such as this would not have to lie about his own country in order to love it, nor would he need a partial and unsympathetic account of another nation, perhaps a competitor to his own, in order to prefer and cherish his own.

Mark Twain wrote in *Innocents Abroad* about traveling Americans. They were, as he describes them, almost delightfully naive and unappreciative of other customs, beliefs, politics, and culture. Not all the innocents in matters of politics have been Americans, however, for we are all mindful of how innocence is really a feature of every group and every individual. It might be apt to say that innocence is the common point of departure for every child. Everybody starts there and that is why innocence and childhood seemed to be so pleasantly linked. Some countries have imposed limits on what their young people can learn, and this often looks as though some of these dictatorships do not really trust their citizens if they should lose their intellectual innocence.

Fortunately, it is becoming increasingly difficult to control all the means of popular education. Today the radio, the TV, and the printed page find their way to people everywhere. Western democracies have usually tried to give access to all the facts to all the citizenry, though in times of stress, this policy has been sometimes jeopardized. It should not be too difficult to see that a major issue in every nation is the degree of freedom to be granted to its citizens, and that the freedom of access to learning and the freedom of the daily newspaper to report the ways of the world are absolutely crucial. A nation whose people are kept loyal only by being kept innocent is paying too high a price for its securities.

Now to return to religous matters. Clearly there is an analogy between innocent religious belief and innocent patriotism. Innocent people do not know there is a viable alternative. In religious matters, this often means that Protestants do not know the strongest case that can be made for Catholicism for this faith is often stated in ways which make Catholics appear to be stupid and priest-dominated. Catholics are sometimes taught that every Protestant is either deluded or is a rebel against order and clearly given authority. Christians are often convinced that their faith is an improvement upon that of the Jews without knowing what Judaism actually is. Also there is a kind of general innocence that is being shattered for Westerners when it is discovered that the religions of the East are sophisticated and subtle, emotionally satisfying, and intellectually tough.

But these general things may not quite hit you and your target. Most likely the reader will have experienced the shattering of his or her innocence more specifically and more concretely.

For example, you may well have been exposed in gentle ways to religious teachings, perhaps by parental example, church-school teachings, perhaps catechism or other special devices, youth groups, plus your sabbath worship. All of it together operates fairly effectively to produce, not always clear and precise beliefs but, certainly, a general orientation and some general views about God, what human life is for, and how one ought to live. Some of us have been taught more than that and with greater detail, and some of us have been taught a lot less. But my point is simply that all of this happened to us in the process of growing up. Most of us did not think hard about it, because we were really being acculturated. And this impressive word describes the odd number of ways by which we are brought into religious organization and belief, almost as we are brought into the family of practices that makes us cultured so that we eat with our fork, wash our bodies, and use polite greetings.

Nonetheless, our faith is then an innocent faith. From the standpoint of religious faith and the Scriptures, I suspect that we would have to say that the faith of the innocents is not the highest kind of faith. While we admit that such faith is all that children can really have, this kind of religious faith is no more impressive religiously than is mass-produced patriotism. Besides, all the examples of great faith in the New Testament as well as in the Old Testament are adults.

So it can be asserted flatly, then, that faith as seen in the context of biblical religion is really the faith of the not-innocent. Among other things, this means that faith must be finally chosen by the individual for himself. It is not enough to have religious faith by virtue of your parents, your priest, or accidents of exposure and society. Rather than religious faith being dissipated by the facts, by the presence of other ways and other beliefs, it must be urged that it is for people troubled by all of these that the faith is ideally designed. Part of the meaning of saying that faith is for sinners simply reinforces this point. To be a sinner includes all kinds of ordinary phenomena with which we are all acquainted. Thus, while sinners do not have to be morally vulgar and downright cheap, it is part of our common lot as mature people to know the differences between good and evil, right and wrong, and still not be able to live rightly. Likewise, when our innocence is gone, we can believe many things, everything from fantasies and dreams to grandiose schemes and pretentious political and social ideologies. In fact, one has to be quite smart even to think up some of the downright silly yet powerful myths that convert men. All kinds of people the world over remember the weird breed of lies and half-truths that gripped otherwise intelligent Germans during the Nazi period, and the history books are sprinkled with an array of equally absurd but still powerful views. Believing in God does not become a very lively belief unless there are some other beliefs worth denying. Again, men make their gods and establish their pretenses over and over again. Part of the business of admitting you are a sinner is to admit that often we too get trapped into such incriminating and falsifying views.

The point to retain in all this is that the Gospel of the Lord Jesus Christ is designed for people who have something to give up, something to be converted from, who are, in short, already sinners. Those who keep their innocence even relatively intact do not know the deep trouble that goes with doubting, with temptation, and with personal despair. For in all of these cases, a person begins to feel a kind of unhappiness that he probably did not know as a child. When you know enough to doubt, you know that there are other beliefs that are likely; when you are tempted, you know that obedience and disobedience are equally possible. When you despair over what you are and what you have done, you perhaps wish that you had been born to wealth or born pretty or been someone else. These are signs that your innocence is lost, and these are also the ways the word "sinner" begins to fit over us. And the Gospel story is tailored for sinners, those with problems and disabilities, dismay and needs. So it should not be shocking then to discover that one's religion undergoes a kind of wrench. In truth, it really is not the religion as much as it is the person himself.

At the outset of our life we believe as a result of training, by parents, and through the community or groups to which we belong. Even the Christian religion is a kind of accident for most people—they are that because someone baptized them, maybe confirmed them, or otherwise instructed and exposed them. Because all these things can be said, it must not be supposed that this way of coming into such matters is trivial. There is a sense in which very mature and thoughtful people can say late in their lives that the reason they are Christians is that their fathers told them. One can be thankful for such a remembrance. Nonetheless, it is not enough; for the world is full of different fathers, and different communities, and unless something besides your father and your community is there to sustain you, you might well succumb to palpitating indecision and shivering doubt. The point is, again, that there is something to be said and to be thought after these early confidences and assurances are broken. Principal among these things is the fact that faith, not least Christian faith, in God and the Lord Jesus Christ as Savior and Friend, true God and true Man, is clearly for mature people.

3. MATURE DOUBTING

If what has been said makes any sense, then it is the case that the early religion which we have been taught must mature before it can be of much use. Certainly it is planted in us by others, but it must be examined and started over as soon as our own need for it begins to grow. Initially we must admit that Christianity has become a kind of bond of the people, and there are few in America who can altogether escape it. There have been other times in European history when Christianity has been almost a tribal religion of whole groups. One need not be very astute to see what the disadvantages are. Some of these disadvantages make up the dark side of religious life, the side that has suppressed minorities, made scientific study sometimes hazardous, and even allied religion and rulers so indissolubly that advocating better government has almost seemed a crime against God.

Again the analogy with governments is rather close. For quite a while in democracies, there has been a widespread approval of dissent. A nation in which no one dissents is more sheeplike than human; and, therefore, most sophisticated countries recognize that even the improvement of government demands a continuing criticism and responsible dissent. It is always a delicate matter to determine where the dissent becomes irresponsible or treasonable. In religious matters, something like this must also be proposed, for the Christian faith must clearly leave room for unbelievers. Whenever a particular belief becomes too powerful an engine within society, bending the dispositions of every man to accept it, we can only hope that it will not succeed.

Our argument has been that a faith that never overcomes despair and doubt is simply not a responsible Christian faith. The difference between childish faith and credulity is very slight. I suppose that we can admit that most children believe because they are credulous—because they do not know enough to ask really hard questions. Credulity is also a characteristic of adults, and there are numerous older people who mature physically but not intellectually. This is not simply a question of I.Q. either. Often we use the notion of the lack of native intelligence to justify indolence and not caring, but it is often the fact that a person does not care, does not take the time, or does not reflect upon himself at all, that accounts for continuing credulity. There is, nowadays, little excuse for even the simplest man not noting the many ways to believe, the difference between good and evil, and the bald fact that there are belief and unbelief everywhere.

One is credulous if he continues throughout his life to believe simply because he was told. Something else must enter the scene. We have noted that it usually does, for young persons are strongly inclined to scoff at patriotism, marriage, religion, and adult sobrieties. I propose here to make this doubting a little more mature. It might even seem that I am advocating doubting, but that is not quite the case; however, there is an issue to be clarified. Most adolescent doubting is downright immature and trivial. A casual acquaintance with an evolutionary theory, a little exposure to a teacher who is daring and a bit radical, a weekend of talk about how morals are relative and just a matter of opinion—these serve to precipitate many doubts. Here again, doubting ought to become a little more serious and even better grounded. And this is what I propose to do.

For example, it is quite plausible to believe in deeply anti-religious views. There are no facts which I know about that cannot be accounted for in a reasonable way by irreligious thinkers. If someone wants to say that life ends with the tucking away of the body in the grave, there is nothing terribly illogical or irrational about that. If someone says the world can be thought about, described, and enjoyed without believing in God, I suppose we must agree. It seems to me a mistake to say that the opposites to a Christian belief are simply foolish views, downright stupid and oblivious to the facts. No, the truth of this matter is that our world is so constituted that alternatives are possible, and one need not be a blockhead to be an unbeliever. On the other hand, one need not be a blockhead to be a believer either.

Our doubts do not become really mature if we are simply griping because of dogmatic preachers, narrow and unimaginative teachers, or even because there were so many things we were not told. Until a person begins to let some of these other possibilities really get a grip upon him, his doubt is very superficial. Again I am not here teaching the doubts or even advocating them, but it is the case that there are very mature and extremely intelligent advocates of irreligious views. Some doubters are like some believers—they are in it rather part-time and for half-baked and casual reasons. On the other hand, there is a maturation in doubting and a sophistication that will chill and sober you as nothing else can quite do. God has never been seen by any man, says a Gospel writer, and that alone leaves room for a lot of doubt whether He even exists. Is He only a figment of the imagination? Is He only what the psychologist might call a projection? Is He only a father-image?

Serious doubting is hard work, for it supposes that the objective uncertainties like those we just noted will be thought about with real concentration. My concern here is to get you to see that there are many objective uncertainties, most of which you can entertain for yourself. Our immature faith was built on what we thought were certainties. Maybe we thought our parents really knew, or our priests and pastors, or our church. While it is true that they know some of these things in a certain way, they are also like you—they have never seen God at any time and they do not have a secret source of knowledge, accessible only to advanced age. The plain truth is that there is no knowledge of that sort and there never was. When your certainties begin to disappear, there actually are no new ones to put in their place. But the point to recall is that Christian faith, though taught to you in such a way that you believed everything was certain, is also compatible with the recognition of the immense uncertainties.

Instead of assuming that religious faith is passé because it cannot be proved, one might at least examine how faith has lived among people who, like John the Gospel writer, will admit that they have never seen Him, yet still believe. Is this only whistling in the dark? keeping one's courage up? Is this really believing in commitment for commitment's sake or because we like and need to be committed?

At this juncture, it might be enough only to admit that there is a difference between credulity and responsible belief. Innocence of all that can be known accounts for the ease with which unquestioning faith can be built into most of us. But the argument in these pages has carried us to the point of saying that the certainties linked with faith were really not certainties, and doubt, after all, is really proper. Doubt is not simply a defect of one's personality nor a result of a querulous nature; instead we must admit that doubt is highly appropriate to the way things are. Doubt is as proper to human beings as their acquaintance with the wide diversity of things and beliefs. Only immature people fail to doubt.

This resolution is a very temporary one however. In the next chapter, we will turn to the kinds of doubt. We will do this in order to ascertain just how the Christian faith accords with doubting and with ourselves in our struggles to gain and to hold meaningful convictions.

Doubt and Knowledge

Our previous chapter made the important point that there is such a thing as responsible doubt. However, there are many forms of irresponsible doubt too. When someone doubts others' convictions for the sake of making light of something precious, or if one is trying only to be a rebel, or if one is psychologically sick so that any kind of belief and trust—in one's textbook, teacher, or the testimony of others—becomes impossible, then we can say that doubt and skepticism are, very likely, not responsible.

Presently, a distinction or two might be of some help. Distinctions are helpful, though, only if put to their appropriate use. Their use is not in remembering the distinctions but in differentiating between kinds of doubts.

The word "doubt" is used for many different situations and experiences. We ought not to be confused by the usefulness of a single word, "doubt," to think that there is something in common between all the instances we call doubt or doubting. Here another example might be useful. If someone asked, "what is exact length?" we might be inclined to look for an answer that would fit all the uses of the term. So, when the hardware-store man asks me: "What exact length of rope do you want?" I say, "Give me twenty-five feet." When I am asked about the exact

26

length of a football field, I say with confidence, "one hundred yards." If I am instructed to measure an exact length of two centimeters, I can easily enough comply. So, in all these instances, I have understood the term "exact length" quite well. However, if someone insists that he would like to know what "exact length" is in and by itself (such that you can have yards, feet, and centimeters in "length"), then we do not quite know what to say. We must know something else; we need an example, since there is no "exact length" that is right for everything.

When talking about our "doubt," the same difficulty might arise. Therefore, instead of rushing to provide a general definition, I want to turn to the examples. Each reader might be encouraged by the practice to rephrase this example slightly to fit himself or perhaps even to supply himself as the example.

2. RESPONSIBLE DOUBTING

Suppose you learned that the Germans were the cause of World War I. Somewhere and somehow you came to this belief. As you study history books, especially those covering the diplomacy of Great Britain and France before 1914, you begin to see that Germany had reasons for being concerned with military power, colonies, alliances with Austria-Hungary, the Russian and the French borders. Your simple view, that Germans were the cause of the war, gets very complicated indeed. Soon you might say: "There does not seem to be much sense in saying Germany is the cause—there are lots of causes." Repeatedly we discover that simple truths, or at least those we thought were simple truths, become doubtful. To say this is to show that we have learned enough to doubt.

That the "Thirty Years War" was a Protestant-Catholic war becomes dubitable when one studies the details of seventeenth-century political life. That the founders of America were searching only for God and freedom becomes a little strained too when the immigrants are better known. Now we can be permitted a little generalization; for it surely is the case that we learn to doubt and to be skeptical whenever we discover that evidence and conclusions do not fit. Sometimes there is no evidence, and then we perhaps doubt the right to any conclusion. Such an assertion as "Hitler is alive in Panama" is at least conceivable, but most of us will doubt it when no evidence is produced. In other cases, we doubt because there is so much that counts, so much evidence, that no one conclusion is warranted, or what is given as evidence does not seem to warrant the conclusion we have been taught.

One of the reasons that doubt occurs with such frequency is that most of our early teaching is the teaching of conclusions. We usually "tell" children all kinds of things, about weather, animals, the past, airplanes, trains, and babies. Most of our early learning easily satisfies our curiosity. And most of us are at least informal teachers for, as parents and friends, we, too, oblige by giving the answers to myriads of questions. It is only a bit later that children discover that almost everything that is said can be questioned. The encounter with evidence invariably comes a little bit later, most often after the conclusion has been learned.

Educationally the situation looks something like this. Initially the children's empty heads are simply filled with what we think are the elements of history, science, and literature. This kind of teaching is very important and essential to everything that follows. But no doubt is encouraged, for the big job here is to get the empty noggins filled. To some degree the same is the case with religious teaching. Willy-nilly, children must be expected to absorb all kinds of things before they can even begin to think about them. If we revert for a moment to the terminology we used in the first chapter, we can say that the intellectual innocence of the child, what we call ignorance, must be vanquished. This is what most elementary education does. We continually must put something—views, beliefs, opinions, assertions—where there was nothing; and we must continually replace falsehoods and half-truths with what we think are the truths.

The next large step in education—and it does not come for everyone at the same time—is the matter of learning to think for oneself. We have all kinds of words for this. We speak of students becoming critical, of solving their own problems, of doing their own studying, or researching the issues, and so on. These expressions refer to the maturing intelligence and the fact that almost everyone can also learn to tell the truth as well as simply repeat it, to discover the truth about something as well as be told it, and to judge the situations for himself as well as being dictated to about them. The faculty for doing all this is a little slower at coming about, and most teachers do not know exactly when and how it happens.

But it does happen. The sign of it is that a kind of doubt and a kind of critical air settles over the student. He no longer wants simply to be told what is what, he also wants to be told why it is so. When this happens, the student has discovered that everything that a person says needs some kind of backing. We usually talk loosely about this by saying that everything needs evidence. And anything is evidence which attests to the view, which gives testimony, which supports the case, which confirms the hypothesis. Therefore, in law courts and in scientific laboratories, we use the word "evidence" in relation to witnesses, to proofs, to documents, to testimonies, to confessions, to circumstances, and to a host of other established particulars. All kinds of odd things are evidence, depending upon what we want to make apparent, obvious, unmistakable, and manifest. For evidence makes something evident, and what it makes evident is usually what we call a truth about something or other.

Most of the time our education, at least of the formal sort in our schools and colleges, is a matter of teaching us truths about something. These truths are usually simply sentences which declare a state of affairs. It is important to see that elementary point, for the truth of which we speak in school circles is invariably a quality and a characteristic of sentences.

Not all sentences tell us the truth. Some are nonsensical, some amuse us, some make us cry, some stimulate imagination, some soothe us, some excite us; and we could add almost indefinitely to the list of the functions that sentences perform.

Happily, language tells the truth too. Consequently, we can write down the sentences in books and preserve the truth, as we say, for future generations. By learning to speak and learning to understand a language, we learn a host of things including, perhaps, the truth. Right here, we begin to see how important it is to have a fine command of language, for with that command grows the capacity to fit words exactly to the intricacies of the world and also the power to speak to the awesome variety of people the world over.

Again some words about our doubts. What most of us discover is that every truth—and that usually is a sentence telling us something—is not obviously true. Scarcely anything is true simply because it is said. Even saying it in a loud voice does not make it true. Every sentence is true, not because it is said but only because it tells you what is so, and what tells you that is it so, is what we call the evidence. A person who doubts is a person who despairs over his thoughts, who finds them inadequate or who does not, at the moment, see that which vindicates them. To discover that all sentences that are claimed to be true still need evidence is a very elementary discovery. But it is also very important, and it never loses its importance no matter how practiced and how responsible a thinker a man might become. Once one has seen this, then one has to learn to look for evidence before one says very much for himself.

Yet, this is not an easy matter. For evidence is of all kinds. When one asks for evidence that "Napoleon was the curse of Europe," one is asking for something quite different than when one asks for evidence for "City managers are more efficient than mayors." It takes a great deal of skill and patience, plus a long exposure to the variety of activities in our world, before one learns to look for evidence at all well. One of the symptoms of intellectual youthfulness is the tendency to make the plea for evidence too general and too easy. Shakespeare's sayings that "all the world's a stage . . ." and "To be or not to be, that is the question" do not yield to this query very well. Poets, too, speak about the world and everything in it, but one cannot address their sentences in too brash a way. If one insists upon doubting all of these because there is no evidence, or because their claims do not appear to be true, there is no easy recourse. Right here is where a lengthier exposure to science, on the one side, and poetry, on the other, is needed before the surgery becomes too radical. Likewise, one needs to live with historical writings for rather a long time before he asks that these be made evident by the same ways that a newspaper reporter might want to verify his story.

All of this may seem an unnecessary complication. But a warning is needed. Much of the doubting that goes on is not finally responsible because one needs to know a great deal to doubt well. I do not wish to blunt the point that I previously made, namely, that it is a discovery, and a relevant one, to learn that everything we believe to be the case needs some reasons and some facts by which the truth is made plain. This is not being denied, and the importance of this is great enough to mark off uncritical students, on the one side, who, though they absorb everything they are told, are finally rather poor students, from those, on the other side, who, though they may not parrot everything they have read or been told, are discriminating and are finally the better students. No, the issue here is very clear. A good student is one who knows that evidence finally makes the case. But it is also conspicuous that there is a variety of evidence, depending upon the issues, the interests, the field, the methods, and a host of other considerations. And one cannot be excited about the evidence, without also caring about the specific subject matter and the respective fields.

The finest thinkers, to whom the rest of us owe the greatest debt, are often people who have doubted all kinds of long-standing views. Isaac Newton, who proposed a single set of laws that described the motion of bodies, both terrestrial and celestial, is a case in point. Since ancient times it had been argued that celestial bodies moved according to laws of circular motion. Simultaneously it was agreed that terrestrial objects could be described according to laws of linear motion. Two sets of laws made motion very complex and Newton long pondered this. It was almost as if there was one order of bodies on earth, another in the heavens, and no way open by which to explain them together. Newton was a great doubter, however, and he eventually dared to doubt the laws about the motion of heavenly bodies. In a masterful stroke, he wrote out his famous laws that fitted both sets of bodies; and he gave substance to the view that there was after all a universe, a single order, not an irreducible duality. It goes without saying that Newton's doubts would have been worth very little had he not known a great deal about the heavenly bodies as well as the terrestrial.

So our point then stands, that there is a kind of doubt that is indeed directed toward our truths. By this I mean only to suggest that as we learn, we learn also to distrust some of the beliefs we have learned. There is a valid and justifiable kind of hesitation and suspicion, one that is born of the recognition that not everything in the world is the way the old wives have said it is. But also it is not as all kinds of us, scientists, teachers, poets, and preachers, have said it is. All of us make mistakes, of course, but more than that, even the best of us in our best moments might have missed some of the evidence. For some of it may have been overlooked, some of it has been hidden, and some of it is brand new. Thus we must learn to sit a little lightly on many of the truths, for only a fool can believe that everything true is already known.

Another way to put the point we have been making is that there is one kind of education which liquidates our ignorance, pure and simple. This is the kind of educating that occupies us most of the time. We need to learn all kinds of proposals as to what the world is and how it works before we can take the next step. The principal psychological feature of learners in this stage is their willingness to believe. They believe easily and well, and the more easily one believes, the quicker the learning. Yet the second stage of learning puts a greater premium on liquidating, not the ignorance, but the credulous and naive nature of the learner. Here we must learn to be critical, to doubt, not because of ill will but because of one's learning. The emphasis is here upon the skills that make one a responsible and skillful thinking person.

We are supposing that this has happened already to the reader. Perhaps this explains why religious beliefs are now so critically examined. Rather than feeling dismay over this, it is being urged that this is a sign of maturing and growing up. Nevertheless, there are some further considerations before one can make doubt truly sensitive and respectful, true to the conditions of religious teaching.

3. JUSTIFYING OUR BELIEFS

Whenever we begin to doubt the views we have about anything, we are approaching the need for justification of our views. I am here using the word "justification" because it is another one of those rich and meaningful words, full of associations with all kinds of important affairs. The intent is to link it firmly with the one kind of doubting we have already noted. In the next chapter we will describe another kind of doubt and also another and related use of the word "justification."

All our truths, indeed all our learning, needs the backing up of which we have spoken. Unless we know what permits and even requires a view, we do not know whether it is justified or not. The search for justification is another way to describe that second level of education to which we have alluded. Rather than always seeking information and more and more facts, well-trained, intelligent people are often preoccupied with the justification and validation of our truths. Several facets of this can be easily noted. For one thing, there is the temperamental difference that goes with such a quest. This is what we have already called doubt, or that air of skepticism, that causes us to seek and to ask, to penetrate more deeply into the subject and to insist upon the evidence. On the other hand, there is, too, what the technical students call simply the logic of the situation. By that we mean only to note that, in almost mechanical ways sometimes, when you have enough evidence, the view itself is true, no matter where you happen to be or what you happen to think. But both sides are involved, your temperament and doubting, and the bearing and the sheer weight of the evidence, respecting the views that are involved.

The quest for justification is, and let there be no mistake about this, a very noble side of being an intelligent and discriminating person. Again the issues are not simple. There are all kinds of ways to justify the various things that we believe. In law courts, we sometimes justify a legal view by citing previous cases, what the lawyer calls precedence. And much of the learning in this field is a matter of commanding precedence. But in other areas the fact that people have thought likewise is not to the point at all. So, in the sciences, it seems that such recitation would scarcely count at all. This does not mean that one way is superior to the other, but only that the processes of justification are quite different. It might be, too, that the doubts were also different, and what is resolved when we justify a doubtful case in law might be quite different in kind when we justify an hypothesis, a point of view, or for that matter, a religious or political doctrine.

But justification is here the topic, and it belongs very intimately to the whole process of doubting. When a view or a truth is finally justified, there is no reason any more for doubting. This is why the intellectual life is really also a matter of great fun. For with increasing skill and knowledge, doubting increases in scope and detail, and then, correlatively, the satisfactions that go with justifying your assertions also increase. Certainly this must explain why intellectual discovery and pursuits are spoken about with such fondness by many of its practitioners. Research and scholarship are quite romantic, in fact, and not at all dull as the early stages of rote learning so often are.

But now it is time to say something again about our religious doubting. For most of us here have learned all kinds of things. They may be general, as was earlier suggested, or they may be as specific as the teachings of the Roman Catholic or Lutheran catechisms, as such confessional documents as the Thirty-Nine Articles of the Episcopalians, as the creed and other bodies of formal discourse often used in much of church life. They may include the words of Scripture and the views of your clergyman and sabbath teacher. The point for the moment is simply that these things too can be doubted and are. It is not difficult to surmise why they are doubted either. For part of the doubting stems simply from asking—"what is the evidence?" And there are difficulties in showing what the justification for these views is, so the doubt grows and grows. There are persons, young people among them, who conclude that there is no evidence and that there never was. Strong-minded and desperate people, such as Voltaire, that eighteenth-century wag and critic, have dared to say that if one did away with the priests one would do away with the teaching. He said this, apparently, because he thought there was nothing else, no evidence, no reasons, no authority, no facts, no situation, no needs, nothing save the priests, which would perpetuate the teachings.

Most persons who begin to doubt religious teachings also begin to discover that there is no experimentation possible with God. There are no laboratories or research centers where God is being researched. Whatever else theological seminaries are, they are certainly not that. And an oddness about things religious grows apace. At first, it looks as though religious teachings are exempt from the requirements we have learned to ask of every other belief; for when we ask for evidence, some religious people are quick to say: "Well, you must have faith." That appears as if there is no evidence and hence no justification for the belief. It seems, then, as though religion depends upon continuing the credulity and childlike innocence that we noted before. Faith, even of the Jewish and Christian sorts, appears a somewhat stupid trait, fit more for old ladies and little children than for active minds.

Something like this appears to be the conclusion of many young persons today about their religious heritage. In contrast to the sciences they are learning, where doubt and criticism seem to be built right into the fabric and process of research and learning, religion seems to be on the defensive and continues to ask for faith and belief. Instead of being aggressive and on the move, always enveloping these newly acquired traits that come to us in our maturing lives, it seems as though religion is repressing the doubts and all the mature reflection and questioning that it brings. Whereas doubting is essential to justifying the views we have learned on most matters, doubting does not even seem to count in religious affairs. In fact, it begins to look as though religious beliefs have no justification at all and that the only thing one can do with them is to believe them uncritically.

But we are not at an end. If matters were left right here, we would seem to say that this somewhat religious skepticism is correct. It is not that the skepticism is wrong or that the doubting is sinful, for nothing so big and sweeping can really be said with honesty. On the contrary, it will be asserted again that the kind of doubting we do of most of the things we have learned, including the religious beliefs, is learned too. That is to say, this doubting is really taught us once we see the gap between evidence and what is being said. Honest, intellectual work and all of the care and concern for facts, for accuracy, for precision, for never saying more than is warranted—these teach us to doubt. Thus, we can conclude that the cultivation of the intellectual life leads us naturally to doubting and to the critical manner that mark a mature human being.

In the next chapter, something more will be made distinct, for we shall there argue that the religious life is also supposed to teach us something about doubting. Just what that is and how it pertains to the issues raised in this chapter will be the burden of those pages.

Doubt and Religion

Admittedly we are side-stepping a bit the issue of the previous chapter. For there we have argued for a kind of doubting that is learned when we push hard into intellectual matters. A certain manner and style is attained—we begin to exercise our wits in a new and exciting way, troubling our elders and ourselves with the provoking quest for the justification of everything that is to be believed. When these queries are directed to religious beliefs, we see a disturbing sort of shuffling, a kind of evasion of the issues. We want to know the proof, and we are often told, "Have faith!" We want to see the evidence, and we are told that we have to grow up. So it goes. Even after admitting as much as the previous pages, it may seem that the approach here, too, is another case of bluffing, one more refusal to face up to the serious charge. Instead of meeting the request, we seem to be floundering a bit, taking on another question altogether.

There is purpose to this, and it is not finally an evasion. For just as the intellectual life creates and sustains a kind of doubt, so too does the religious life create and sustain doubt, although it is another kind. Before we can engage in the contest fully, we have to ask something about the religious teachings—what they do and how they are related to the religious life. We will discover and hopefully define rather clearly another kind of doubt actually produced by religious practice. How this becomes entangled with the substance of intellectual doubting will have to be shown, and the hard questions can once more be addressed readily enough.

2. DOUBTING OURSELVES

For the moment, we must think about religion, and especially the Christian religion, in a very inclusive fashion. We have referred repeatedly to religion and often meant the Christian doctrines or what we earlier called the sentences that purported to be true. There is, however, much more to religion than beliefs. Christianity is also represented by churches, by liturgies, by sermons, by prayers, by moral attitudes, by a host of practices, convictions, priests, pastors, parents, and programs. Accordingly there are numerous ways to become, to be, and to remain a Christian. One learns Christianity, indeed, but that can mean that one obeys Jesus' commands, says one's prayers, feeds the hungry, preaches the good news to others, loves his neighbors, and all kinds of other things.

Most of us have had some kind of exposure to religious practices and teachings. It may be the sabbath worship, perhaps liturgies and sacraments, or it may be somewhat less dramatic and plainer worship of only hymns and sermons. But the point is that this big range of stimuli, everything from plain words to songs, architecture to music, orations to homilies, are also teaching devices. All of these conspire to do something to the individual, and what they do can be called a form of teaching. One learns to be polite by imitating others, by accommodating to the situation, by becoming at ease in novel circumstances, as well as by a host of other procedures. Becoming religious, not least in the Christian fashion, is something like that too. This is not to deny the importance of beliefs, but it is to draw attention to the incontrovertible fact that one also has to learn to be charitable, hopeful, faithful, kind, patient, and humble.

Not altogether incidental to this level of learning is a certain attitude one begins to assume toward oneself. Perhaps we might say that this is an understanding of oneself; but that word "understanding" makes the matter sound too theoretical and too intellectual. So "attitude" will perhaps do it better and we will use that expression. Let us take one or two examples. After one has been singing for a long while (and I mean here, for example, since childhood or over a span of years), "Holy, Holy, Holy, Lord God of Sabaoth," the effect of such singing seems clearly to magnify, as the expression goes, the Lord. And when He and His name are thus made great, it soon dawns that very little of that hymn is in praise of oneself. Church worship and private prayers also cause one to kneel and to prostrate oneself. Simultaneously, God's name and His works are being praised. Another example is the oft-repeated expression, variously used in public and private worship, "Christ have mercy upon us." Again with much reiteration in the appropriate context, there is a kind of learning that is altogether appropriate, and this learning is the recognition and acknowledgement of oneself as needful.

On the one side, Christian worship and literature proclaim holiness, love, mercy, single-mindedness, and strength, but primarily as the characteristics of God. In several forms, there is the teaching that every man is a sinner, that each is in need of a Savior who can wrench him from his bondage, set him free, and remake him into God-likeness. Again, though, it is well to remember that even apart from explicit teachings, the religious practices themselves induce humility, something of self-denial, and what one might without exaggeration call a restrained self-doubt.

This phenomenon of self-doubt is sometimes, if not always, an indirect product of religious life and worship. For here is not the kind of thing one absorbs on a weekend or by reading one book. Neither can one say that learning this self-doubt is a matter of repeating a few verses of Scripture or a doctrine about original sin. This self-doubt is surely another kind of doubt, not a doubt of the truth or falsity of sentences, but a doubt concerning the validity of oneself, one's character, wishes, and purposes.

We might put it boldly by saying that most of religious worship and practice is calculated to induce an appreciation of what is a diagnostic fact about oneself. The expression "diagnostic fact" needs perhaps some explanation. A fact is diagnostic when it permits one to diagnose a troublesome situation. Not all facts are diagnostic and not all people are able diagnosticians. Simply knowing the facts is not enough to qualify one as an able diagnostician. This is true respecting even the most elementary and crucial facts of one's own person. Oftentimes we have intimate and personal knowledge of our own illnesses, but we lack the ability to spot the diagnostic fact that will permit the remedy and cure. We readily hire others, our physicians, who will spot those diagnostic conditions and enable us to do something about our illnesses.

It has long been said that religion is the medicine of the soul, and since Jesus' day, there has been wide acknowledgement that the priests and pastors function as doctors of the soul. However, these terms are a little obscure, not least the word "soul." Instead, let us suggest only that no one seems to be born healthy of mind and spirit. The symptom of this is that no one is happy except with rather strenuous consideration and even effort. Though it is very easy to admit that one is unhappy, it is often very difficult to diagnose the unhappiness, namely, to discover the cause and to suggest the conditions for happiness. However, the world is full of helpful people. There are happiness merchants by the score. Literally thousands of proposals are offered almost daily.

Because physical ailments make us unhappy, health seems to be the necessary and sufficient condition for happiness; and there are nostrums, everything from patent medicines to physical exercise that are proferred to us. Others suggest that we need money and the more the better. Again, poverty clearly contributes to unhappiness, so we easily conclude that plenty is the answer. All kinds of other remedies are available too. We are tantalized by "charm," by education, by social position, by the Ivy League, by a long life, by a companionable marriage, by sexual experiences, by the ability to speak well, by all sorts of fulfillments of desire and stimulations to our lagging desires. Most of us chase happiness almost like the will-o'-the-wisp, always uncertain of its whereabouts and its appearance among us.

It may seem out of order to suggest that the Christian faith joins human beings at just this place, but it is the case. Actually, it is not unorthodox to say so, though for some reason it is presently a little disreputable to link happiness and faith, perhaps because of the large number of religious leaders who therefore pretend to be happiness merchants themselves. However, the religious quacks ought not to defer us from admitting this point. Most religions, including Christianity, are not direct ways to happiness at all. This is the mistake that some people have made in fomenting religious interests, though it must be remembered that there have been people dealing in problems of mental health who have done the same thing. We all know mentally healthy people who are unhappy, and mentally unhealthy people who are happy. To say that one will be happy if one is mentally adequate is to make mental hygiene and care a nostrum too. Thus in religious circles, the fact of a kind of unhappiness and an almost nameless sense of inadequacy and need surely drives people to the churches, but it is too easy to say, therefore, that religion is only a means to happiness.

Nonetheless, here is the occasion for understanding the coupling of our unhappiness and the Christian religion in its many facets. For it is the express contention of the Christian heritage that men are indeed unhappy but also that the teachings of the world, as to what we should do about it, are simply mad. However, it is not the case that poverty, pain, and ignorance are to be laughed at or that their power to increase our unhappiness is to be denied. Here there is a funded awareness that Christians must also share. But the remedies are what need the scrutiny; all the while it cannot be disavowed that money, health, and education relieve all kinds of disabilities. Thus, Christians too will seek these with and for the rest of the world.

But the primary condition for happiness the Christians have always seen to be something of a secret and a strange secret at that. It is one of those open secrets, not something intentionally hid from others or something too mysterious for most people. It really is not even secretive the way a profound truth of science might be, known only to those who are properly qualified by long discipline and skill. Christian teaching and practice conspires to make us aware, even if it is painful and very uncomfortable, that we ourselves are at fault. The condition for the pervasive unhappiness is within the man, not outside of him and not simply in the conditions of society and nature.

For this reason, the Christian's participation in public worship is designed to bring him to the admission that all is not well with him. This is the self-doubt of which we spoke earlier. In place of self-confidence, which too easily lays the blame for one's unhappiness on other conditions, on misfortune, on one's ugliness, or one's stupidity, there is a self-doubt that biblical teachings convert slowly yet firmly into the sense of sin. Then one's own guilt is admitted, and the fault is seen to be in oneself, not in others.

A variety of ways of eliciting and describing this condition is available. "Lord have mercy upon me, a sinner" is one of them, but there are others too. The Christian churches and literature juxtapose each of us against some very trying commandments. Even those known as the Ten Commandments are very difficult to obey. For example, honoring your father and mother is a lifelong task and one is, therefore, never done with that requirement. A few occasions of forgetting one's parents and one begins to acknowledge his guilt for not obeying the command; and the command does not need the repair as much as does the person. The admonitions of Jesus have much the same effect, for He says that a man who looks at a woman with lustful intent has already committed adultery in his heart. Clearly that does not omit many men, if they take His words seriously, from the uncomfortable awareness that they are not as pure as Jesus suggests. Many more examples could be cited too, all of them illustrations of the fact that learning to despair of oneself, to doubt oneself, is certainly the necessary condition that Christian discipline marks out for a happy and fruitful life.

In the second chapter, we have noted how a kind of skepticism, responsible and measured to be sure, is absolutely essential to thinking intelligently and well about our world. Not least is this true because the world is so full of ignorance and of plain lies. It takes great and continual struggle to winnow the true from the false, the true from even the plausible half-truths. But in matters closer to us than intellectual affairs, there is even more fraud and deceit. The irony is that we do not have to be deceived always by others here, for we are our own deceivers. There is a continual drive in most of us to declare our self-sufficiency and to lay the burdens of the world at other points far from ourselves. The contention of this chapter thus far has been that the teaching of the faith, though not simply a doctrine or a belief, is in the direction of softening up the hard heart that others, and of fixing responsibility and guilt in the inward man not the external conditions.

It must be admitted that this kind of self-doubt is taught almost incidentally and indirectly, not directly. One can no more teach this directly than one can teach intellectual doubt directly. It will not do to teach everyone to be skeptical and not so credulous by teaching them some big truth. Would it not be odd to say that "everything is doubtful, therefore be skeptical"? For if you were skeptical, you would have to doubt that saying too. No, the way to become a reasonable yet skeptical person, who knows when to doubt and when not to doubt, is by long cultivation in the ways and practices of gathering evidence, formulating your thoughts, and seeking the relevant facts. So, too, in religious matters, the way of coming to responsible maturity of holding yourself blameworthy and guilty is not through a general teaching, but rather through long exposure to religious practices and worship. The aim here is not agreement with the view that everyone is a sinner as much as it is knowing when and how to hold oneself responsible for the fortunes and course of his life.

Therefore, religious life itself diagnoses the human unhappiness by insisting that every man is guilty, is a sinner, and that this condition must be addressed frontally before happiness and peace, contentment and poise can be expected. In short, this is the diagnosis proposed by Christian teaching of an all-too-human situation, the perennial state of our disquietude and needful lives. Human life is most often a continual and restless search for satisfactions. When one thing fails we try another, then another, and on and on it goes, without ceasing, our entire life. It is part of the boldness of Christian faith to say that the teachings of this world are here radically wrong, for they invariably accentuate the illness rather than cure it. We become more restless and more difficult to satisfy the more we accomplish and the more we succeed in doing.

The net effect, then, noted to this point is that the Christian way supposes that one must correct the perspective upon himself before he goes any further. He needs the cure and remedy before the rest of the world gets its reform and renewal. To doubt the validity of the self that you already are is not an easy matter, and it takes concentration and remembrance, a willing disposition and a contrite spirit to make it happen at all. But certainly one major theme ought now to be clear. There is a great difference between doubting a thought and doubting yourself. The first is described as being skeptical, when one is no longer sure whether a thought is adequate to the things it describes; the second is described as being in despair, when one is no longer sure whether one's life is adequate to the demands made against it. Most of the time we would never be aware of the inadequacy of our thoughts unless we exposed ourselves a bit to the heights and depths of intellectual work. Likewise, most of us would never be aware of the inadequacy of our lives unless we exposed ourselves to some demands that were a little out of the ordinary. Just as a good school does the former, so a good church, along with the Bible, does the latter.

Learning to doubt and to be conscientiously critical is an indirect effect of our ordinary education. It happens, nevertheless, only to some people, not all. The efforts of churches are also only partially successful, for only some people really become contrite and humbled people, admitting their need for grace and renewal. The self-doubt of which we have spoken is rare perhaps not because of the lack of talent or the lack of exposure but rather because this doubt is like an admission of defeat. No one likes to admit his defeat. Hence we seem to evade by all kinds of odd devices this kind of disclosure. This is perhaps the reason church services are so different than schools. Every day is different in our school life, with new subjects and new areas constantly being introduced; but church is much the same from week to week, and novelties are just a little suspicious. The aims are different; in schools and colleges more and more learning is the goal, but in church the admission of a very few things, getting them firmly etched in the human heart, is the principal objective.

3.   BEING JUSTIFIED AS PERSONS

The demand that all of us make of our intelligence is met when our thoughts are justified. To justify a thought is to show that it is warranted by the evidence. But there is another use of the word justification too. In moral and legal circles, we show that someone is justified if the circumstances exhibit the justice or rightness of a person or of his acts. Or by showing that a person had good cause for his conduct, we adduce the grounds which justify him. This means in brief that we do not hold him blameworthy.

But in theological and religious circles the use of justification has been still different. Two familiar contexts have been proposed: justification by faith and justification as a special theological proposal whereby a person is declared free from the penalty of sin because of Christ's righteousness or of the infusion of grace. These two uses are, of course, closely related and, in part, allude to the same range of considerations. But the point to which we want to direct our attention is not, as yet, the theological belief but rather the interest and concern that self-doubt produces in us. Hence, the concern here is how this kind of doubt of which we have spoken motivates another kind of justification.

It is clear enough that a false or an unwarranted hypothesis stimulates most of us to seek a true and warranted one. Therefore, there is something very proper about seeking a justified conclusion from the evidence. What we justify by evidence and by argument is only our knowledge about something or other. This kind of justification has its rules and methods, even a kind of logic which can be learned. But there is this other kind of doubt—this strange anxiety and dissatisfaction—that we have also learned by becoming mature people.

Little children seldom show us anything quite like this, for children go from one bauble to another, picking and choosing their way with careless glee. As long as there are enough toys, enough games and playmates, the daily round is pleasant. But with a little aging, things become quite different. Adults become aware that there is more to living than these little distracting asides. If ethical seriousness has taken root at all, so that being good is a matter for concern, then there is no end to the self-reflection. Furthermore, if one has any smitch of conscience, even the fleeting wisp of awareness that everything in heaven and earth can be considered under the canons of good and evil, right and wrong, then it becomes all too plain that all is not well, every moment at least, with oneself. To this extent, scarcely anyone is immune from some kind of self-doubt. It, too, is natural—as natural and, in its way, as easy as pride and self-regard. Like the capacity to doubt what is commonly said and believed, so, too, the capacity to doubt what is commonly accepted and what passes for ordinary human living can be cultivated and strengthened.

One of the functions of church is to strengthen and to nurture this kind of self-doubt. Just as we noted that intellectual discipline makes doubt discriminating and just, so, too, does spiritual cultivation make one's personal despair responsible and pointed. It is a mistake in teaching to give everybody the results without giving them understanding of the nature of reflection. They must realize that the results come after the torture and the joy of thinking hard about matters. Few people are able to assimilate results without being rather stupidly dogmatic. The man who thinks well knows that the results are tentative and only the best to this date. Likewise, it is a mistake in the religious life to offer people the peace and the contentment without the tears. Putting it flatly and in religious terms, it is a mistake to suggest here that one can have the joy without the repentance. First, the task in Christian circles is to teach everyone to make their self-doubts both accurate and deep enough. They have to know doubt by their own doubting—they have to know this despair by their own despairing. There is no substitute for this state, for this is maturity. Without it a person stays superficial and trite.

Both of these kinds of doubt, cognitive and personal, emerge in the life history of people. They are among the signs of maturing. Both of them cause us to seek justification, but of radically different kinds. One of the confusions, seen usually in bright young people, is the assumption that everything in religion and ethics depends in some obscure and round-about way upon getting the ethical and religious views and beliefs fully warranted according to intellectual criteria. Something of that is probably present in these requests to "Prove it!" But there is a corresponding confusion among others who, recognizing the great importance of justifying and improving the quality of one's life, still are very apt to believe that this justifies all of their views as well.

A separation has to be made. Once it becomes clear how necessary it is to become a good person, to obey commandments, and to live a useful and worthy life, one is started on

another and never-ending process of justification. Here the
enterprise is one of ethics and Christian faith. Here the person
himself is unjustified and found wanting. Sometimes we feel
ourselves guilty because we have not done what we know to be
right and just; sometimes we find ourselves inadequate and
weak where courage and strength are expected; sometimes we
discover that we cannot even care about the things we say we
love and cherish. Certainly in these conditions there is a striking
need for a kind of self-justification. We want to be guiltless,
right, and just; we wish to be courageous, strong, and adequate;
we would like to love and cherish and be worthy of being loved
and being cherished. This is why the need for a justified life is
ineradicable and a sign of our humanity. Only a fool would not
let this need possess him.

We are not here proposing any great novelties, for most of
these things have been noted long since; but the arrangement of
them might well be new enough to waken some sluggish thoughts.
Since time immemorial, one of the principal functions of moral
teaching has been to perfect men in the direction of refining
their deeds and their conduct. It has been commonly held that
much of ancient Hebrew religion and the works of the law were
designed to justify men by a more perfect moral life. Again,
whether we have ancient authority for such a prospect is of little
moment, for each person finds himself often trying to live in a
way that will be legal and right, guiltless and good. Most of us
do not need much prompting to do this, and one of the strongest
motives for doing what is right is certainly that this will soften
the judgments we make of ourselves and that others make of us,
too. Much that we describe by an anxious conscience is also
relieved and atoned for by our good deeds, and all of us know
about that by virtue of first-hand experience.

All kinds of extremes are also open to us. There are people
who will not do any good deeds unless some publicity is promised; and such people look as though they were seeking justification in the court of others. The apostle Paul is another very
extravagant example of a person seeking justification, and he

says several times that he was most zealous for the works of the law and that consequently his obedience to the law, his works, were more marked than many of his critics had surmised. He speaks very volubly about this feature of life almost as though the law itself cursed him with a quest for a justification he could never attain. There are others, too, who do not strive so mightily but who take refuge in the thought of being average, and try, therefore, to find their justification in being like the rest of the race. These again are sometimes called "realists," but here of a moral sort, who are inclined to accept the human lot pretty much as is and leave it the same way.

There is something very profound and very revealing about a man's preoccupation with ethical concerns. Very few people are content only with their cars, house, and family. Most of us also want a big cause to serve and a few moral victories somewhere along the line. We want and need some enthusiasms and passions that are the sort of which we can be proud and which will redound to our honor. On that account we begin to assess our life, hoping that it will have warranted the love we got, the wrongs we did, the time we spent, even the life we lived. Surely, in some such loose way as this, most of us hope our lives will be justified. If we were at fault, then we want to rectify the fault by perfecting whatever remains to us to change.

The Christian story is addressed to this same set of circumstances. However, it changes the scenario somewhat. For, as we have noted, it, too, like the ethical economy, causes us to doubt our present state. It puts a stress upon the need for the transformation of the individual. More than this happens, too, for instead of asking us simply to view ourselves in our own perspective, or in the light of society's demands and laws, or in the context of morally great personalities, the Christian environment educates us, even trains us, to criticize ourselves in the light of a holiness and a perfection that is described as God's. In return, the stakes become even higher. The guilt we acknowledge is described as a guilt before God, and this begins to deepen the sense of guilt. The inadequacy is measured by a holiness that is far greater than general social expectations. This is what religious training does. It makes very firm and very inclusive the sense of impotence and powerlessness, almost to the point where one begins to despair altogether.

This may seem a reckless and foolhardy kind of teaching. There have been critics who have heaped scorn upon Christianity for encouraging such seriousness among us. But all is not lost, and those critics who say that it is are probably seeing only one side of the matter. It is true that Christianity encourages a sense of loss, an utter want of expectation, and an almost complete loss of hope. However, the key does lie, finally, in the unapproachable excellence of God, which is more responsible for the Christian's despair (as Bunyan's *Pilgrim's Progress* notes), than is the badness of the Christian himself. And the excellence of God, though deepening the self-doubt, is also the ground for the new hope. The rest of the story, as well as the rest of Christian practice, lifts that load by declaring that the justification of every man is in God's keeping.

"Justification through faith" is the Christian slogan. There is a point to placing this expression in contrast to "justification by works"; for this is how the phrase became current in ancient times. Justifying persons is still our big theme in contrast to justifying language and truth-claims; but this justifying of persons may be either by acquiring ethical qualities or by faith. One can suppose that "works" here covers a large span of moral factors, everything from motives, dispositions, and feelings to deeds, programs, and law-obedience. Christian literature always relates Jesus of Nazareth to every man by saying that though He is not simply one more moral teacher telling how to achieve the serenity and peace, yet He is pertinent to everyone in need, not least those who are heavy hearted and burdened with guilt. So it was to the self-doubting and despairing ones, the hopeless ones, that He came. It is little wonder that morally immature people, those who are self-assured and prideful, as well as most children, can make very little of Him, other than that He is one more interesting teacher and seer.

In the Christian literature and in most church worship where His birth, death, and resurrection are celebrated, His life and teachings acquire another function and relation to all people. It is there taught, again not only by doctrines, that He is both the justifying agent and the actual justification of sinners. Persons are urged to look upon Him as their hope, almost as if they can be relieved of their desperate and almost dangerous hopelessness, by His life and death. It seems that many people actually did take hope by being in His presence and doing what He said, and of this we have ample testimony in the early historical sections of the New Testament. Others have remembered His life and deeds, through reading the Scriptures and hearing them recited again and again, and much the same sort of effect has been seen. The apostle Paul and others have summarized much of this in classical terms, now called theological by saying that He is our justification, He is our ransom, He is man's hope and the propitiation for our sins.

Christianity is here making a very strange proposal, one which Luther says was not clearly thought up in the kitchen. Most of the homely lore that is thought up in the kitchen is rooted quite obviously in what we have already called the ethical way of thinking. Most of us will easily conceive of another kind of rightness, or what religious tradition calls righteousness, that will satisfy our deep longings for a justifiable life. But Paul's writings and other Christian teachings, the hymn writers, and the very shape of Christian worship with its emphasis upon Jesus' life and mission, combine to tell us that our justification is only in Christ. Even our righteousness, glowing as it might be, is said not to be quite enough to justify us, not unless, of course, one's standards are low enough! Again if one's standards are as high as the church says they ought to be, then the need for Christ also becomes clear again.

In a classroom where the average brings the grade of B, even the A is not necessarily a major achievement. And in the context of Christian worship, the standard is pushed very high, so high that it is said that all are sinners and all fall short. Such a standard is the glory of God. It is against such criteria that even the popular worship in the church pushes every worshipper. No wonder then that self-doubt is created in that context. Self-doubt and acknowledging oneself to be in need go hand-in-hand with this kind of justification that is also personal and nonintellectual.

4. THE ISSUE FOR CHRISTIANITY

To conclude this chapter it is essential only to point out that there are at least two established orders in which doubt and justification play their part. We have noted how intellectual doubt can be a sign of a very discriminating and responsible person, fully alive to the peculiarities of honest thought. Here the pursuit is for justified conclusions and for justified arguments. Nothing has been said to belittle this kind of interest. On the contrary, to become learnedly skeptical is to be more perfect. But this is not the only kind of perfection we need.

Every one of us is also in the business of becoming responsible people. Our lives are subject to other demands. We must learn to be people of character, to have habits that are really virtues, and to make ourselves approvable, if not to others, at least to ourselves. This is the other arrangement in which doubt and justification play their role. There is small point to dwelling upon the similarities between them, for we can easily be misled into thinking that both are expressions of something invisible and very spiritual indeed. These pages have cautioned against that kind of interpretation. Instead, the reader has been urged to think about the differences between them and, if at all possible, to take each seriously on its own terms.

As must be clear already, this has not been a plea for Christianity. Nothing has been advocated, except some elementary reflection upon the issues. Whether anyone wants to become a Christian depends, to this point at least, upon whether or not anyone wants or needs justification on the terms we have noted. There are, surely, other considerations that can be advanced, but they have not been urged here nor even presup-

posed in any mysterious way. Instead, this effort has been entirely directed to seeing just what the issues are.

If someone says that he or she doubts the truth of the Christian faith, it at least is appropriate to point out that Christianity,
too, teaches a kind of doubt. The best grounds for rejecting
Christianity are not these somewhat vague doubts about its
truth but rather that one has concluded that it does not do what
it sets out to do. The Christian faith is not primarily some more
information or one more view—it is not another hypothesis or a
kind of peep-sight on the universe. If it were primarily these,
then it would have to be judged on strictly intellectual grounds.
In that case, all the queries we apply to scientific views, to
opinions, and to popular views would certainly apply. Primarily,
Christianity is addressed to the issue of people saving their lives,
making them count up to something. This is why Jesus is called
a Savior and a Redeemer, something we would scarcely dare
call our local teachers. Christianity thus appeals to our need
for a personal quality that is resilient and tough, that will survive scrutiny and criticism.

It is on such a ground that Christianity ought to be accepted
or rejected. This is to say that Christian worship and practice of
course include all kinds of teachings, some of them quite difficult to believe. But the stick must be picked up at the right end,
and the theological teachings are not the right end of the stick.
The right end, the place to get hold of the business and to
understand, is how Christianity fits at all our common human
existence. It does fit, if one brings into the open his own misgivings about himself, his own shortcomings, and his deep dissatis-
factions with himself. Whether or not it fits any further—for
example, whether it fits one's preferences and wishes—is altogether another matter. Whether it will really do what it promises
is still another issue.

Before one answers those questions, one should be very sure
that he has seen what the issue is. A good part of the issue is
whether or not one has been taught anywhere, by moral discipline and even elementary concern, to doubt his own status and

character. If he has, then he is perhaps eligible to consider what Christianity proposes. If he has not, then it might be better to admit that he is in no position to discuss the faith at all.

Maybe this seems too jaunty and easy. We must remember once more the person who says—"Prove it!" Those teachings about God, creation, and salvation seem terribly abstract and almost fantastic. If ever doubt seems to be due, it seems altogether fitting and suitable right here. After everything is said, we appear to be back where we started, with the question of whether these teachings are in any wise justifiable. In the next chapter we shall try to show how the issue as seen thus far begins to apply.

Knowledge
and
Religion

Instead of satisfying those who want answers that cannot be doubted, we have shown that there are two kinds of doubt. One kind, very important to our intellectual interests, does find its relief in answers. And these answers, in turn, can be properly doubted only as we learn more. Therefore doubt becomes one of the main features of being intelligent, for it acts like a dissatisfaction which drives us on to a better resolution. Furthermore, this doubt never ceases and, in brief, is one reason that thinking has been called dialectical, meaning that it moves from doubt to relative certainty back to doubt as the evidence demands. So much for answers.

We have made a case for another kind of doubt, too. Here there are no answers, for the aim is not an answer as much as it is a plan and a proposal, a way to resolve one's life. Therefore, it is a little absurd to seek answers of the intellectual sort in this arena. Tentatively we can say then that Christianity is not designed to satisfy our thirst for knowledge or to resolve our doubts concerning the truth or falsity of our intellectual schemes. Christianity feeds on another need that each of us has, the need for a justified and approved life. The doubt, that is despair, and the justification, that is our salvation, are as different from doubt and justification in intellectual affairs as Christianity is from science and scholarship.

55

To separate these concerns is very easy to do on paper, but hard to do otherwise. For these two kinds of justification and doubting become thoroughly jumbled in our daily lives. A token of this is the oft-repeated theme that many people strike, namely, that their intellectual doubts have actually cut their attachment to religion. They are far larger in number than those whose interests in intellectual matters have been severed by an interest in Christianity or Judaism. So the matter is a serious one. People, perhaps the readers of these pages among them, do say that their doubts make Christian belief impossible.

Some readers might say: "According to your arguments to this point, if faith justifies people and religious doubt is primarily a self-doubt, then there is nothing to doubt. But we do doubt something, usually the Bible or some other teachings. What about them?" In short, it might be said that we have not made a case as yet for theology, for it is very likely theology, or some specific view or other, that we doubt when we say that we doubt our faith.

It is time to admit that Christianity is not only a set of habits, a style of life, a way of feeling about things, a psychological and temperamental matter. For Christians also believe in doctrines and hold some truths to be important for all the world to know. Our question will be how these beliefs can be related to what we have said about doubt and despair.

It is time to assert, too, that there is something called religious thought. Not least of what we have learned in our churches might be part of that heritage of Christian reflection; and Christian reflection is deeply indebted to the Jewish heritage and other powerful influences too. But Christian thought, like religious thought in general, is of two broad kinds. On the one side there is a kind of thought "about" faith and everything connected with it. This thought is knowledge and is like all other knowledge, subject to doubts and to vindication and justification. There is, though, another kind of thought, and this is the thought "of" Christianity, a language "of" faith and not, strictly speaking, "about" it. This language "of" faith is the heart of the teaching of the churches. How it relates to our self-doubt and to our justification, and how it relates to the cognitive doubts we have already noted, will be a good part of our task in this chapter.

2. SCHOLARLY RESEARCH

There are all kinds of bits of knowledge that have been long associated with Jewish and hence also with Christian beliefs. For example, as one reads the Old Testament one discovers that the tribal peoples we call Israelites were once slaves of the Egyptians. According to the stories in Exodus these Jews were, like most slaves, the victims of all kinds of injustices, but eventually they found their leader, Moses, who, amid incredible hardships and wanderings, led them toward another land. All kinds of odd things are reported about their wanderings. For example, they are being led to a "Promised Land" because this land, flowing with milk and honey, has supposedly been offered them by God, the ruler and owner of every land; they find water in a cleft of a rock which, as the hymn reminds us, is in "a weary land." Moses and Aaron subsequently are somehow responsible with God for Ten Commandments, which thereafter become a kind of covenant God has made with the people.

One could go on to cite numerous other stories, like these, intimately associated with Christianity and Judaism. Because Moses, David, Jesus, and Paul were historical figures, not figments of the imagination, there are numerous things said about them that are of the kind that we call historical assertions. All sorts of events are reported, everything from births to floods, battles to miracles, and all kinds of activities are described, from the sermons of Jesus to the wanderings of apostles over the ancient world sites. For long centuries these many claims have been simply intertwined with all kinds of other things making up the religious literature, and very few seem to have been especially inclined to balk over their inclusion. Church practice and popular teaching of the faiths have kept this miscellany of literature in an almost intact form, teaching it all pretty much in the religious interest.

Only within the past century and a half or so have sharp discriminations within the religious literatures become popular, though, in fairness, we must admit that many of the distinctions we shall note here were drawn sharply by first-rate minds much earlier. In any case, it is relatively recently that sharp separations and a systematic and scientific study of certain of the materials have been proposed. Part of this new kind of study stems from methods learned in the studies of nature, whereby men began to formulate descriptive laws of natural events in new and daring ways. Other techniques were soon developed for assessing the truth of historical views. As the eighteenth and nineteenth centuries moved on, new crafts for treating these religious materials arose. No longer were men content merely to repeat what ancient authorities said, even if they were eye-witnesses, for moderns also wanted to know whether what they said was true or false. Gradually the very documents of the past were questioned, their age, their authenticity, their truth, and a host of other characteristics. Much of this is what we know as historical criticism, and the Bible as well as other ancient texts were thus rather quickly and thoroughly canvassed in these new ways.

Matters were soon pushed even harder. For if the texts are authentic, there is still the question of the truth of what they report. Some convictions probably sustained by the kind of science that Newton did when he formulated laws that described the motion of both heavenly and terrestrial bodies began also to operate among students of Holy Writ. It was not long before readers began to wonder whether all of nature, past, present, and future, was not of one piece, too. Perhaps the so-called laws were really laws of all nature. If so, then the sharp separation of divine events—miracles, creation, birth by supernatural means —from human and nonmiraculous events became also a little dubious. Applying the framework of conviction that was slowly accumulating from the sciences gave all kinds of people pause about the sort of miracles reported in the Scriptures. Perhaps these doubts, well described in the literature of many critical thinkers of the relatively recent past, are not too unlike those that are felt by many readers of these pages. It was only a short step to saying that the story of creation was only a story, nothing more, and that most of the other unusual events associated with God and Scripture were fantasies and myths of an earlier age.

Another kind of critique developed, too. This had to do with the truth of very specific historical claims made within the documents and within the living tradition of the church. It was not long before the massive accumulation of stories about the activities of the saints, the fates of the blessed dead, the shroud covering our Lord, these and more, even the specifics of the New Testament, were subject to quite serious inquiry. This was historical research, turned upon the life of Jesus, the history of the church, the origin of sacraments, the sources of the liturgy, the derivations of beliefs, the very foundations and springs of the popular teachings of the churches.

It ought to be noted here that not all criticism and doubt is recent. Since earliest times there have been doubters in the context of the Christian churches and the Jewish synagogues. What is recent are the remarkable ways that we have found of making some doubts responsible and sometimes even fruitful. Most of this kind of doubt is what we will here call "cognitive" doubt, that is to say, doubt about the truth or falsity of what someone claims to know. The upshot of this doubting in our day is an awesome accumulation of knowledge. And the accumulation today is simply tremendous on matters associated with the Christian faith.

We are the heirs today, therefore, to a vast fortune of knowledge about Jewish and Christian faiths. This has come about because of all kinds of new research, new ways to make materials speak, and techniques and devices scarcely dreamed of in earlier times. There has been, consequently, very remarkable progress in the sheer quantity of knowledge as well as its comprehensiveness and precision. Never before have we had such general social skills at work in digging up evidence and making it count.

This is to admit that doubt of this cognitive sort has flourished among all kinds of peoples, including every nation of Europe and also in America, simultaneously with the quest for better-justified and warranted views. The upshot is plain to see. We know an amazing amount about the history of ancient peoples including Israel; we know a great deal about the early Church and its vicissitudes; we know much about the origin of certain books of the Bible, about several authors of those books, and about why there are differences between them. Almost any large library will quickly show you a range of literature, much of it a consequence of careful research and assessment of arguments and evidence, that is a new sort of knowledge about all kinds of phenomena associated with faith. Even the language of the ancient literatures has been scientifically studied, along with the customs of the people, the varieties of their convictions and the changes in their views. Not even Jesus has escaped this careful study, and every fragment telling of His life and ministry has been scrupulously gleaned, not once, but many times.

So then there is a kind of doubt, cognitive as we now call it, that is amply taken care of in the modern world. If anyone wants to know about philological, historical, archeological and, broadly speaking, textual matters, the chances are very good that such doubts can be met by this huge quantity of knowledge. There is little reason for curiosity being unsatisfied any longer. There are numerous centers of research and almost countless scholars today who are doing first-class scholarly and scientific work on the literary and historical materials connected with the Christian faith.

But there is only one small matter to be remarked upon, and

that is simply that most of this scholarly work does very little to reward another kind of doubt. For if one is doubtful whether Jesus was God or whether God made the world, there simply is no comparable research going on in those areas. Very probably it is that no one knows quite what would count as evidence or even where to look for it if you did think you knew what would count. Something like this is also the case with the issue of God's existence; for here we have a host of arguments (not, strictly, very much that looks like evidence) for His existence, but most of them are not very persuasive except to persons who are either very sophisticated so that their problem is no longer the plain one ("Does He exist?") or to those who already believe for other reasons.

The aspect to be noted here is that most of the scholarly research of our day, and make no mistake it is considerable, that pertains at all to religious things, is clearly "about" religion. It is not "of" it. People who are religious do believe some very crucial matters, such as that Jesus was God and that the world was created by God. These assertions are typically made by people who are religious. They are not found otherwise. They are not the kind of neutral and objective truths that are enunciated and believed independently of one's religious constitution and orientation. The claims of science and certainly those, too, of history are seldom in any wise dependent upon what else the scientists or historian says or is. If they were that, they would not be science or history. In fact, the point we have made all along is that there are a large number of truths that are truths simply in virtue of the evidence, and the evidence is impartial and objective, there for all to see and to know. But we do not have evidence in quite this way for the kind of peculiar theological claims we have noted. No one is quite ready to specify what the evidence is or even where it is so that one could find it for himself.

This is the reason, then, for saying that a certain number of beliefs, for they are sentences which someone believes to be true, are not really amenable to the very scholarly kind of justification the world has increasingly learned to provide. Nonetheless, they are very important, for they are typical of people who are religious. These striking sayings are part of the doctrines, the systems of beliefs, in which we have been schooled and to which we are exposed in church practice and worship. If doubt begins on these, we are at a loss to suggest precisely what to do. Accordingly, doubt flourishes.

I was bold enough earlier to say that a certain kind of doubt was a sign of maturity. But here we do not want to make a virtue of unbelief or to give skepticism too high a rating. Nonetheless, it is true and therefore must be said that it is not an answer to someone who doubts the kind of sayings that are really theological, namely, that he must simply have faith. For one cannot sit down one day and start to believe them. If one has learned that there must be evidence and there is no evidence, then believing comes very hard indeed.

On the other hand, there is little point to blaming anyone who doubts these teachings, for it is not in being blamed that one will find his way to certainty. In fact, the conclusion also previously made was that doubting, even religious teachings of this theological sort, was highly appropriate. Now we can see why. For there are no easy ways to fit some of these theological beliefs over the facts. It indeed does look as though some of these beliefs are sufficiently unrelated to the facts, or whatever they are about, that one cannot look at those facts and determine the truth of what is said. This is what we mean when we say that these doctrines are uncertain, when considered by reference to the objective facts. No more peering at the data, no more assessment of the argument, really resolves our questioning.

This somewhat strange turn of affairs means, too, that there will be little purpose in pursuing endlessly more details in the learning about religious matters. For there our curiosity and our doubt are sooner or later resolved, at least if we have asked decent questions and looked at the available evidence.

But the next thing to do is to look more closely at some of

these doctrinal and theological assertions. It may be that a closer examination of them will tell us what they are and how they work for us.

3. WHERE RESEARCH MAKES LITTLE DIFFERENCE

Modern ways of doing research have clearly multiplied our stock of knowledge about almost everything associated with religion and the Christian faith. Therefore people who doubt a whole range of things, about Martin Luther, John Calvin, Jesus Christ, King David, about the history of the books of the Bible and the authenticity of legends and stories, can have that kind of doubt lifted from them. But there is another range of issues that cannot be studied, and therefore doubt does not cease here; instead it grows steadily unless it is stopped by some other suggestion. What is that suggestion?

We might make here a very elementary distinction. The knowledge that all of us have to some degree about anything you please is written down or spoken in a language. That group of words can be English, French, Latin, or what-have-you. But one thing is obvious, that language is all "about" the world and its many things. We have said that there is also plenty of language that is "about" everything associated with Christian life and beliefs. So we can and do have language "about" believing, "about" doctrines, "about" Jesus, and "about" even the advantages there are in being a Christian.

Language "about" religion is not, however, quite the same as a language "of" religion. For it is also the case that some language is an expression of religion and is not only about it. The distinction we want to press here is that between a language "about" and a language "of" Christian faith. It might well be that the conditions for learning one such language are quite different from learning the other. Also the conditions for doubting one are very different from the conditions for doubting the other. Before we move to these issues, we ought perhaps to pause on the distinction itself.

An analogy might be in order. Today most of the forms of human loving have also been studied in great detail. Everything from the details of sexual life to the forms of marriage, from the physical cause for affection to the social causes for divorce, have been studied in the greatest particular. Libraries house books on the love life of civilized and uncivilized people, early and late, as well as numerous studies of the love life of animals. So here, too, there is an immense language about love, almost matching that about numerous other important concerns. Scholars can do all kinds of research here and answer any number of questions and resolve all kinds of doubts. If someone wanted to know whether it is true that two can live cheaper than one, there is ample enough information on even the economics of married life to lay that saying to rest. One's chances at a successful marriage can be judged in the light of a surprising array of statistics about people like oneself, and we can predict, crudely to be sure, even a little bit about possible success and failure.

But it would be quite another matter if someone wanted to learn how to speak the language of love and to do it lovingly. For the language of love on one's own lips is a very fragile and lovely bit of speech. When it is appropriately said, it becomes one of the performances of love itself. People who are in love speak lovingly and kindly to each other, for their language is an important way to sustain and even to create the affection. But there are no courses to be taken on this subject. There are plenty of courses and books about love available in a large modern university, everything from the sociology of the family to the economics of marriage. Even the course in the most gifted poet of love would not, however, be the means of learning to speak lovingly. Someone might be fooled for a while by the pleasant trippings of one's tongue, but after a very short while, most of the beloveds would want to have those expressions of speech in your own tongue and in such a way that it would be clear that love was there all along.

So, anyone who wanted to speak the words of love could surely listen to others and he might buy all the anthologies of love letters. He might even hire someone else to write his love mail for him. But none of this is quite the same as learning to speak lovingly. Think how hard that is! On the other hand, think of how many people have learned to do it without any vast learning or any major research. All the courses in the catalogue of the biggest school in the world would probably not help very much, if you did not begin with loving. But we are a little ahead of our story.

Let us return to the issue of religion once again. There is surely such a thing as the language "of" faith as well as the one "about" it. Probably it is true that the way to becoming religious is not by taking courses about religion, though they might clarify the issues and settle a lot of strange questions and doubts that we had had for a long time. Still, how does one learn the language of religion?

Perhaps this seems too simple to be taken seriously, but most of the language of religion is learned almost as we learn the language of everyday life—by exposure. We may be exposed to it in the hymns of the church, in the liturgy (which is the language of faith in a kind of dramatic form), in the Scriptures, and in the sermons on scriptural and other topics. But the principal source for the language of faith has always been Scripture itself. Every page of it is saturated with religious fervor and enthusiasm. A kind of passion seethes through its stories and parables, histories and letters, that marks it off as a quite strange book. Nonetheless, this is not the only place one finds the language of faith being spoken, for every Christian who has any gift for speech at all, must surely occasionally speak faithfully just as lovers must speak lovingly. Without the words on one's lips, one is a somewhat odd lover, and so, too, in matters of Christian faith.

Another way to draw our distinctions is to say that there is today an immense knowledge available about Christian things. This knowledge is by and large rather new. It is a consequence of research and all kinds of new disciplines and sciences. Because it is knowledge, it can usually be described in familiar terms as history, as philology, as archeology, as psychology, as sociology, and so on, for all of these fields and methods of study have been extended to religious and Christian matters. All of this is what we have already called a language about the things of faith. The knowledge we also have which is psychological, sociological, historical, and so on, about love is also "about" not "of." Our point has been all along to say that this literature (or knowledge or language) has all the uses of any kind of knowledge. It satisfies our curiosity, makes things clear that were obscure, and, not least, it fits very well the doubts and critical intelligence of a maturing person.

We ought to pause here to remember what an achievement this accumulation of knowledge is. Just a few decades ago, there simply was no knowledge except hearsay available on many issues. If you look at a modern book on the archeology of ancient Palestine or a contemporary book on the history of the early Christians and then compare these with what was available to people one hundred years ago, you will see for yourself what progress in learning means.

However, there has not been the same kind of progress on more intimate and personal matters at all. For we do not mark progress in the language of love as we do in the language and knowledge about it. Scholarship has moved forward very rapidly on the study of love, of political life, of religion, and of all the ways of human behavior. In all these areas we inherit the knowledge and are better off for it than were our parents and their parents. But it is not true that political convictions and loyalty to one's country have become easier because of the new sciences about political behavior. Neither is it true that it is easier to be a faithful and loyal husband than it was before there was so much knowledge about marriages.

This is why then we have made a rather sharp distinction between knowledge or language "about" and language "of" Christian faith. A modern high-school student, who has read a few books of religious scholarship, might actually know much more about religion, even Christianity, than his elders (especially if he has been fortunate enough to read very good books). Sometimes this advantage that young people now have—and it is an advantage—makes the young people in our high schools and colleges impatient and scornful of the older generation, who might not be quite so modern and up to date.

The skepticism and doubt, of which we spoke earlier, that are so characteristic are not necessarily deeply responsible. For as was said, responsible doubt is the kind that is nourished on knowledge. This means that one at least ought to have read some books and thought quite a bit before one talks too critically. But much of this doubt becomes a habit that spills over to every area of human life, probably because doubt and skepticism seem to be built right into our best modern teaching and learning.

The plea made in these pages has been to make our doubts responsible, and we can surely do so with all of them that involve knowledge, evidence, facts, and research. But, it is also true that part of the strange learning in human life is learning to speak lovingly so that one's words themselves will be the means and the expression of love. Likewise, if we choose to be Christians, we must speak faithfully and Christianly so that our words will not be about faith but of the faith.

Oftentimes our doubts are not very discriminating or what we might term selective. But it surely is the case that much of what we doubt in religion is really the language of faith, not the language about it. If it were always the latter, the solution would be simple enough—we then need knowledge and a better-justified view. But if we doubt the language of religion, what do we need? I suspect that often it is not evidence or more knowledge. We might then need to learn to live, to repent, to think about oneself more concentratedly, much as the original users of the language we are entertaining also did.

4. THE HUMAN POINT OF VIEW

What does doubting the language of faith involve? Lovers who have kept their affection through many trials of a married life will often find themselves talking to each other in ways that are a little strange to outsiders. An example can be supposed. If a man had lost his job and is deeply hurt and discouraged, it might well be that a loving wife could whisper to him—"Don't be so blue! Things aren't so bad as long as we have each other!" How are things? Every one of us can imagine poverty and what it would be like to have no hope. Perhaps some of us can imagine, too, what it must be like to see the whole world, one's past and one's future, in the light of a very strong and ardent love. Lovers might well say—"Love conquers all" and then keep their hope up, or they might say, "What's there to complain about? We are exactly where we were when we first met, and remember how happy we were then!"

But it is possible to conceive of a man so deeply disturbed, so chagrined, so hopeless at losing his job, that he would this time, at least, refuse to be consoled and would, therefore, persist in his despair. Then the words of his wife might seem like so much palaver, a kind of whitewash that he would not want at all. He might even get angry and tell her to stop saying these same things over and over, that he had heard them before, but this time they simply were not true. Now what could the poor wife say? In his dismay the man may accuse her of falsehoods, of not seeing things the way they really were, and may say that surely facts are facts.

This is the way a great deal of important talk goes on among us. Here there is a question whether the issue is going to be resolved and the despair of the man alleviated by making him calmly address all the facts of the case. Is full and complete knowledge what he actually needs? Sometimes it might be that things are not serious. Maybe he has forgotten that he is close to retirement anyway; so what difference does one year make? But if his wife says to him, "There is one thing you have forgotten, and that is how much I love you, job or no job," then his forgetfulness is not so much of the facts as it is how love really works. It is not forgetfulness of a knowledge sort—not the kind when we forget the correct answer, or the sequence of kings, or the capital of South Dakota; instead it is a forgetfulness that is more like a lapse of your good manners or like an inappropriate display of emotion and we say—"I'm sorry, I forgot where I was."

Nonetheless, a man who is angry over the turn of events will often begin to doubt the language of love. Some desperate people then see the whole world differently. It seems to be the world of one's enemies and one says all kinds of things about it. Great lovers usually do not find the world to be such a bad place, and the language of love is usually quite able to take death and suffering, and all the other hard cases, quite in stride. Who are the realists here? Who deserves the doubt? Is this only a matter of a point of view?

People who say that all that matters is your point of view are already cynical and rather thorough doubters. The loving wife, who insists that things are not so bad, and the angry husband, who says that things are a lot worse than anyone knows, really believe that they are only talking points of view. They believe firmly that they are talking about the way the world actually is.

The language of Christian faith is like the language of love and yet different from it. For Christians gradually are being taught—if they are at all good learners—by the liturgy, hymns, Scripture, and sermons, to render the whole world in the light of their faith. The language of faith, like the language of love, tells how everything in the world is. Thus far they are alike. But Christian language—and here we include the great beliefs— declares how all of this is when we refer everything to God. Here the languages are perhaps unlike.

If someone doubts that God made the world, is his doubt actually based upon some new evidence that has lately turned up? If someone doubts that Jesus is God, is his doubt actually based upon some subtle anthropological material that has been accumulated about numerous tribes who have believed in Messiahs?

Certainly many doubters of religious doctrines will say that this is the case. Perhaps it is true that some people are initially puzzled about their church's teaching when they learn new cosmological views and a host of other matters. But there does seem to be a confusion here, for often there is no clear analysis and description of what is involved. For too long doubters here have been told only that all these doctrines are revelation, or that you simply have to believe them no matter how you feel about them, or that the Bible is literally true in all details and cannot include any mistakes anyway. Somehow, these assertions are almost crude and, besides, they do not work.

On the other hand, it is not my purpose to credit every kind of light-minded and trivial criticism that pops into anybody's head either. For the matter is serious. Sometimes it seems that the rapid growth of knowledge and the interesting and effective ways we now have of teaching it have gotten a bit ahead of our churches and religious practices. We have become almost swamped by the growth of learning and the language about everything. We need to pause over the importance and role of these other kinds of language and the other ways of handling the world that they both represent and are.

For it simply is not true that evidence would settle the differences between the wife and the despairing husband. One is no more realistic than the other, if one means by realism a regard for and attention to the facts. Neither is one more idealistic. The chances are that both of them admit the major facts, and they cannot convert each other by a recitation of something they think is evidence. Everything counts on both sides, and that is the trouble and reason that the dispute cannot be easily settled.

What is at stake here is not only the difference in what they say about the way things are, but also the big difference between the spirit and qualities of persons that say these things. The disagreement is not only in what is said but in subtle differences in the selves who say them. Not for the moment can we agree that therefore the views they enunciate are only personal confession or their points of view. Nonetheless, the only hope for their agreement with one another is probably as the wife says, exercising her often-tried patience: "Don't argue with him. He will come to his senses. I know he loves me and he's only angry now."

Christianity describes men as if they were victims of a kind of madness of this world. They are all caught up with interests and loves, hopes and wishes, that come very easily, almost naturally. Amid the very exciting stream of life, most of us build up our self-confidence and keep strengthening our powers by education, by successes of all kinds. Most of us develop a certain kind of toughness that gets us through even a lot of hard spots. Soon we are looking at the world according to what we might call a thoroughly human point of view. And this is no secret, for all of us are rather good at it. We want more pleasures than pains, more successes than failures, we want to be loved along with doing some loving, we would like to leave our mark and make life a little better for our children.

Often enough it seems that the world will permit these things, and so we begin to state how it is. Maybe we have to cheat a little, not be too scrupulous, not too demanding or severe with ourselves; for as we say to one another: "That's the way life is." Perhaps it is not necessary to give any further examples on this point, for all of us have heard people say how the world is. We get used to a lot of this talk, the language of this world, after a while. We become accustomed to thinking that cheating, war, small injustices, half-heartedness, and the enmities of people, slander, backbiting, and hate are normal. When we discover how helpless our efforts are to repair all of this injustice and organized unhappiness, we are again inclined to say, with an air of resignation, that that's the way it is.

The teaching of the Christians is radically different. Here, too, we are told what the world really is, and the churches of Jesus Christ go on and on saying and doing pretty much as they have always done. Certainly one can understand that many people become impatient with the sameness of the Christian enterprises. But, for the moment, it might be well to ask what the churches are doing to us and for us. A point we made earlier becomes pertinent once again right here. It was said that the many-sided activities of the churches also taught us to doubt ourselves. For in the world we live in, we still try to justify ourselves and make ourselves approvable. We not only win our

Brownie points but we strive for all kinds of other advantages and favors all our lives.

In this context which is so familiar and plain, the context we make every moment of our life, the Christian ways are calculated to shake us up a bit. Unless we see ourselves as somewhat dubious and in need of a justification that is greater than we can ourselves provide, we cannot even find God. Once one has begun to admit this kind of self-doubt or to practice this kind of thorough despair about oneself, then the large Christian beliefs begin to work for one. Christian literature is our teacher here, not only for the beliefs but also for the depiction of the kind of people we must be to believe these things. The apostle Paul is a good example; for he said very grand things about the whole world and God that are the very rudiments of theology and he also showed us what being a contrite and humbled man really means.

This is as much as to say, then, that Christian doctrines about God and the world, those we have learned in creeds and catechisms, are really language of the faith. Therefore, they are certainly about God and the world, but their truth cannot be judged simply by reference to God and the world. Thus, questions of their evidence and their justification take a rather strange twist, however, not too different from the turn that we noted earlier with the angry man and his loving wife. Certainly it is not believing them that makes them true, but they still are believed to be true, otherwise there would be no point to believing them at all.

The question is, what does cause people to believe them if it is not evidence? The fact is that there is no negative evidence either, nothing that really counts against them. Again the analogy with the distraught man who knows the facts and the wife who knows the same facts is pertinent. The facts alone are not enough to account for their big differences in belief about the way things are. So, in the Christian arena. If someone doubts the Christian teachings, it might be that he really sees the world from his human point of view. And this point of view is not something trifling or cheap. Actually it is almost inescapably human, neither of little consequence nor slight in any way. Christianity positively attacks this customary, and what we believe is the only, point of departure. It hits us where we are vulnerable, by attacking our confidence and self-reliance.

The consequence is an entirely new outlook and a completely new and radical set of judgments as to what the world really is. The teachings of faith are those new judgments. No one has said here they cannot be doubted. Indeed they can. But the grounds for doubting them are finally not some special knowledge, a new science, or some startling data, but rather the familiar human vantage point which we all have so easily.

It is the customary and habitual, the average and the ordinary, that starts our doubts of the truth of Christian beliefs. Just as a lover has to keep his passion coursing within him to survive the shocks of daily life so that he does not lose his perspective and confidence as to how the world is, so, too, does a Christian have to keep reordering his self-estimate and his related enthusiasms and interests in order to keep his confidence from slipping into black despair.

Certainly there is doubt, but doubting the language of faith may be a matter of not having discovered the truth about oneself. Christianity tries to teach us that we are sinners, despite the many appearances and many strengths that are to the contrary. When we admit that we are, a whole new vocabulary and way of grasping the world becomes ours. This is what the language of faith finally is. The major theme of this chapter is to the effect that those teachings "of" the faith will only be fitting and proper when we become proper and fitting, that is, when we change ourselves, our passions, wishes, and hopes. With this change, the teachings also become not just about us, but of us, and, indeed, about everyone and everything else too.

Theological Beliefs

After our inquiries of the following pages, there still may be questions as to what these theological beliefs are and what they do. By this time it should be clear enough, too, that no easy answer will be provided. The general intent of these pages has not been to provide answers as much as it has been to turn the thoughts of the reader to the problem of handling the issues. For often, more answers could mean more doubts or, at least, more sentences to doubt. We have been interested, instead, in why the doubts arise in the first place and, accordingly, what kind of doubts we have been dealing with all along.

We began by noting the familiar fact that most of us start believing in God almost as we do most other things, by being told. If we have honest teachers who respect their pupils and who love the truth, too, then there is no great difficulty. Most of us learn all kinds of things by the help of such teachers. However, we used words a little strangely in order to describe this kind of teacher-learner situation. It was said that the pupils were "innocent," and this because the students did not know enough to doubt the teacher's words and because there were no alternative ways open to thinking about the issues at hand. People are said to be credulous if they believe this way through their entire lives. No one ought to mistake the shape of his early life, for even though we do ask a lot of questions, still our early history is one of believing most of what we are told. This holds for our religious training too.

Then the doubts start to come; and they come partly because we learn about evidence and how many ways that almost everything can be put together. The more we learn, the more we tend to question, and once again the knife-edge of our doubt is soon put against religious beliefs and practices too. Instead of regretting this, we have been supposing that this is often healthy and almost inescapable. Along with such doubts, though, also grows a general brashness, a kind of youthful boldness, that makes many young people (along with quite a few of their elders) very willing to criticize anything associated with tradition, with restraints upon novelty and independence, and with authoritative people and institutions.

It is ironic, almost humorous, to remember that our new funds of knowledge do not only satisfy our curiosity but also create all kinds of new doubts, because one has to know something in order to doubt responsibly. Therefore, it is true that a modern person learns to doubt almost as he learns his subject matter. Along with this intellectual doubt, there is also the kind of doubt that is closely linked with our personal unhappiness. For as we mature, it has been argued, we also begin to wonder whether we are all that we ought to be. A Christian environment specifically causes us to think about our imperfections, about everything that makes us quite unlike God, who is holy, just, perfect, and beyond compare. Therefore, our self-doubt becomes a kind of self-despair, whereby we learn to seek another and better quality of personal life. Of course, this does not happen quite as it is here reported. It happens often in church, sometimes in the confession of sins, sometimes when we think hard about ourselves and our future. If one takes seriously religious biographies, it happens in a thousand-and-one different ways.

Two kinds of justification loom up—one is the kind we know when we verify, prove, and confirm a hypothesis or a theory or a law; the other is the kind of justification that we seek in an exonerated and good life. Our point is a simple one, namely, that the Christian faith is in business to justify lives of men, and this is clearly seen when it is remembered that Jesus Christ died to justify and to save sinners, not to justify or to save hypotheses or theories.

Now we have been led to see the differences between doubts and between different kinds of justification. But the question still nags a bit—how can we believe these religious teachings? Can one believe the Bible? As was noted, too, there is today a sizeable body of knowledge "about" the things of faith, so there is no excuse for accepting anything that happens to be said about these matters. However, there is no such easy way to resolve the questions we direct against the teachings "of" the faith. And it is these that still may bother us.

In this chapter, we will turn to another consideration of these teachings. Here we are particularly concerned with the sort of thing that cannot be verified by scientific methods, that are the very rudiments of Christian belief. What must we say of teachings about the creation of the world, about Jesus being the Son of God, and a host of other matters? Granted they are "of" the faith, what difference does that make?

2.   THE WAY OF BELIEVING

Again we must introduce a somewhat odd usage for perhaps what is a familiar word. The word is "consciousness." Our proposal is that everyone has "consciousness" and is "conscious," according to a fairly clear and understandable use of these words, when he intends the world. But obviously no one sits down to intend the world. That expression is, thus, a kind of shorthand, standing for a variety of things we do. For example, when I smile, squint, or gesticulate at you, when I cry, laugh, or speak, when I work, play, and eat, then I am conscious and I am intending the world.

Our purpose is not to use the word "conscious" in such a way as to make the reader believe that it means only having an idea or having awareness. Certainly our proposed usage might include but it does not demand these. An example might be in order. A child was one day exploring the new house into which the family had moved just hours before. There were no carpets on the floors or the stairways. All of a sudden the toddler slipped backwards down a long flight of stairs and hit her head rather soundly against a plastered wall. She lay inert with the anxious family around. But of a sudden, the mother said: "She's conscious, she looked at me." In a moment or two, everyone was certain of the fact that she was conscious, for she smiled, wanly to be sure, and then she took the hands of others. Of course, she may have been aware too, but it was quite enough to note her smile, her looking, and other bits of behavior.

Nothing odd or highly mental or strangely hidden is being referred to, then, by the word "conscious." When a man is sitting idly letting the world go by we might say: "He seems to be unconscious." When Susy does not kick when you tickle her foot, we wonder whether she, too, might be unconscious. On the other hand, if a person is almost restlessly alive, responding to things here and there, scarcely letting anything go by without a response, we speak about him as being conscious of everything about him. The child who cannot sleep because of being so excited by everything is a case in point. Someone who responds to the beauty of the sunset, the loveliness of the clouds, the sorrow of other people, the humor of all kinds of situations— this person is wonderfully conscious.

The point in alluding to these words "conscious" and "consciousness" is to remind ourselves that Christianity teaches us a way to be conscious. That means that Christianity requires of us a special way to intend the world and all things in it. So being religious is also learning to laugh over the right things, to cry over deserving matters, to care about others in certain ways, to follow our Lord's example of not respecting some people overly much because of their station in life, and so on. The point is that being a Christian does not require of everyone "consciousness" if we mean by that being aware of or having ideas about; rather it does require us to love our neighbor and to live unto others as Jesus Christ also did.

Sometimes it is said that there are two main groups of the Christian churches, one group liberal, the other conservative. Perhaps every reader has heard one or more churches described this way. This distinction has been drawn sometimes to point up that liberal Christians want to emphasize the ethical teachings, the commands, and perhaps much of what produces the kind of consciousness we have noted above. Then, being a liberal often means liberation from some of those difficult theological beliefs that one finds in creeds and Scriptures. Christianity, consequently, seems to connote a very special way of being good; and, in turn, anyone who is especially good is often called a Christian even if he or she does not believe very much in ritual, creed, and so on. The conservatives, on the other hand, are those who emphasize the theology and the Scripture, and they seem to insist upon believing the teachings, the Apostles' Creed, and the Scriptures, for example, as a sign of being a Christian.

This distinction seems to the author to be false as well as unfortunate. But we must admit that this way of thinking and speaking is very well established in many Christian circles. It is hoped that another way of thinking about these issues can be here proposed, using the idea of the Christian's consciousness as our point of departure.

Our point is that the education of a person in the Christian way of life is not complete until he begins also to change his ways of handling the world around him. For he must judge the world differently if he is a follower of Jesus, he must even see it, use it, as well as think about it as though it were God's world. Therefore, all kinds of strange behavioral differences are to be expected. For example, one takes a little lightly the judgments of others; one no longer uses time carelessly and stupidly; one finds everyone else to have a kind of claim against oneself, even if he or she is dirty, an enemy, and utterly stupid. This is what is meant by saying that there is such a thing then as a distinctive Christian consciousness.

The issue between so-called conservative and liberal Christians is false because it makes some people believe that being a Christian is only a way of behaving. Others seem to think it is chiefly a way of believing. If our argument is correct, being a Christian is a matter of both behaving and believing, not one without the other but both together.

Sometimes young people are taught the teachings in a very bald and unimaginative fashion, and they respond by repeating the main theological themes almost by rote. No one wants that to happen, but it does, partly because of the manner of the teaching and the somewhat placid and responsive character of children. Other times, and often informally, we learn by a kind of osmosis what is expected of Christians, namely, that one should be kind, nice to old people, and generally perhaps like the priest or the minister. Now, however, an advance might be made, by suggesting that ideally the Christian teachings should accompany a growth in Christian consciousness and that Christian consciousness, in turn, should require also the specific Christian teachings.

For without learning to intend the world as a Christian, most Christian teachings are really superstitions. If someone mouths them, repeats them over and over, and never lets them change his way of behaving, those teachings actually become myths for him, a kind of idle story, neither requiring nor producing anything except the language. Or, if someone studies the language of faith and continually tries to penetrate its mysteries and simultaneously forgets the kind of consciousness that is supposed to go with it, the language of faith will become metaphysics. And metaphysics is, among a lot of other things, an attempt to see into mysteries and declare what the world actually is. Or, if one likes only the words of faith rippling over one's lips, so that their very sound pleases the ear, then they may well become nothing but a kind of poetry, again without any ethical substance and without the power to remake one's life.

Our charge is that whenever Christianity is taught us so that all we get is the teachings, then, of course, doubt flourishes. For those teachings then seem to be superfluous, almost a meaningless babble of words. It is no wonder that many persons come to doubt them, for they seem to have no great work to do. On the other hand, if all we have learned are the mores and group behavior of our church or the general advice as to how to be good, then Christianity seems to be a rather poor competitor to the Peace Corps and to other modern ethical energies in our society.

Consequently, we can affirm that Christianity is not just a matter of attitude and behavior, or what we have called a form of consciousness and a way to intend the world, nor is it only a matter of beliefs, theology, and the teachings of Scripture. Thus it is a mistake to assume that the teachings are only designed to produce the behavior, so that once one has learned to act as a Christian then one can forget the teachings. This is what some avid people contend when they say that it does not matter what theology one has, so long as he acts like a Christian. Others are inclined to say that it does not matter much how one behaves providing he believes the truth. Instead of all these we are reasoning for the view that there is an intimate relationship between the form of consciousness—how we handle the world—and the teachings. Our responsibility is to make those teachings fit our lives and our lives the teachings.

We have argued all along that theology is actually the language of faith, of your faith and mine. However, the task of teaching that language must begin by teaching it as the language of someone else. When we read it in the Scriptures, that language is clearly the language of the Gospel writers, of the Psalmist, of Paul, and of the rest of the scriptural authors. We can rest assured that it is the language of their faith. In our mouths, it is a third-person language, not quite a first-person singular language. As time goes by, and if we are well nurtured in Christian ways, it might also become a first-person mode of expression.

3. THE RULES OF FAITH

Here a great deal is asked of course. For most people when looking at the language of Paul, of the Psalmist, and of other exponents of faith (and for that matter of the church and its official teachings) want to know simply whether it is true or not. Most of us might grant all that has been said thus far and yet will balk at just this juncture. It seems so natural to say: "But I want to know whether what they said is the truth. If it is true, then I'll believe it too." And doubt then comes home to roost.

What is more proper than asking about the truth of beliefs? But this is precisely the point. If what has been said makes any advance at all, it is that it is really improper to raise such a question here simply because it is raised in this way about so many other topics of interest. Even though one is very serious and very troubled, still the seriousness is no guarantee that the question or the doubt is proper and that everyone else is unintelligent or stubborn if he refuses to respond quickly.

And this is not to say that Christianity is terribly complicated or that only exceedingly smart people can understand it. The fact is that the language of the church—the teachings all of us have found strange and difficult—is initially the expression of somebody's faith but not of our own. We are taught it and, by and large, we must learn it by rote and repetition. We hear it, sing it, place it in our church experience, even become accustomed to it, and sometimes also like it. One day, perhaps in our youth, we begin to wonder if it makes any sense; and our doubt has then begun. Is there any recourse?

Earlier we noted that another kind of doubt might also be growing up. If we are beginning to wonder about our vocations, if we have deepening misgivings about our wasted years of school, if we do not seem quite smart enough to do what we ought, then we might be on the brink of the kind of self-despair that makes Christianity begin to mesh into our lives. What before was an abstract and vague teaching might now begin to spell out the details of our lives; for Christian teaching tells us that when we are most honest with ourselves, when our judgment is most clear and without guile or deceit, when we admit what we are, then the teachings of faith begin to include and to explain us very well. Though it is a step, it is not a long step, from understanding oneself to be needful, and not quite what one has assumed heretofore, to saying that one is a sinner in need of God's grace. Mind you, these two judgments are not the same, but to say the first prepares for the second. Without the first, the second is almost empty and even doubtful; with the first, the second begins to acquire meaning and becomes increasingly relevant and certain.

Here we are insisting then that the language of faith becomes less dubious, less doubtful, only when one plays the game of life according to the rules of faith. One of those rules is simply that one must do the work and deeds of faith before one knows the truth of the doctrine. One must learn to intend the world as a Christian, one must acquire slowly, with all of one's dispositions and indispositions duly considered, the consciousness of the Christian. This means that the language must become an expression of one's own faith and not only remain the expression of the faith of the scriptural writers or of your parents, teachers, or pastors.

Some readers might leap to the conclusion that now everything is clear. Christian teachings are only expressions and nothing more. If a man says, "Ugh," we are usually inclined to say: "What's the matter with you?" for, most of the time, such a word tells us more about the man than it does about whatever he happens to be looking at or thinking about. Often when we talk about language being an expression, we are quick to assume that it reveals and expresses the user's feelings, his point of view, or his or her life. Now this is not being denied in the religious context. Indeed it is the case that Christian teachings are certainly expressive, and they are supposed to fit and to express your feelings, point of view, and even your inner life.

Our argument has been that to be anything less would make these Christian teachings more like science, where feelings, points of views, and the inner life are quite an embarrassment. For none of these count there, and most scientists and most scholars of whatever subject matter try very hard to free their language of such ingredients. At every crossroad on our path, this issue has been met, even to the extent of our saying that self-doubts stir up the interest in the justification of oneself—this much and more of ourselves is always involved.

To add this other point is, however, to mark a great difference for those expressive teachings; for Christians also dare to believe these teachings to be more than a point of view and an expression—they take them to be the truth about God, the world, and anything else to which they refer.

Once one begins to speak as a Christian, one tries to make the language of the faith, probably as reported in the Scriptures and the teaching of a church, also one's own. To do it by absorbing more and more of it naively and in a credulous way is to perpetuate that childlike innocence of which we have already spoken. To do it by repeating it at length and crowding every question out is to become superstitious. To do it by making the teaching so subtle and so profound that it means one thing to simple people and something else to very smart ones, is to deceive oneself with much learning. Some people dare to think that the problem is surely in the language of the faith. They argue that it is now too old fashioned for modern people, too alien for persons at home in this new twentieth century. Our theme has been, instead, the rather simple one, that the language is perhaps quite all right, but that what needs changing is the person.

To make the language of faith one's own is not a matter for a single hour. Here one must take seriously all that otherwise goes into making one a Christian. The other teachings of Jesus, his difficult requests, his strong commands, plus all the other media of worship and liturgy, church discipline and character-forming factors, these and more, are also terribly relevant. Most of us need to learn to love our neighbors, especially if they are un-lovable, before we can begin to say that God is love. Most of us need to become carefree about the tomorrows before we can even dare the thought that God will take care of us. Unless we give up caring so needlessly and in such a worrisome and fretful way, we do not stand much of a chance of ever saying that God watches over us and will guide us to our salvation. In strange and yet powerful ways like these, the person is changed really to fit the language, so that that language becomes an actual per-formance of his faith, not only a reminder of it in others or the promise of it for oneself.

Therefore, to doubt the language is one thing, common enough to all of us who are teachable. But the aim of most things in church, including the language of the faith, is to start us off right by making us doubt something else, namely, our-selves. The doubt that brings the teachings of the church into the right perspective is that despairing kind of self-awareness which is the sense of our inadequacy and need for reintegration. That doubt is the right one in the context of Christian doctrine and Holy Writ. If we start with that, the promise seems to be that we will be able to fit the rest of the doctrines to the world and to God as the need arises.

In the preceding chapter we alluded to the man who had lost his job and who therewith concluded that everything was dismal and dark. The wife, you will remember, said that one could not argue with him but that he would remember that she loved him and that he would subsequently see things aright. The language of faith bids fair to being the way the world and God is when you see things aright. If one remembers what he himself is—a sinner in whom there is deceit and little good, beset by tempta-tion, inclined to a good he never does, and doing what he seldom approves—remembering all that, then one is asked to believe in God who will start one anew. There are many ways to believe "in" God (not just "about" Him), and one can start from a variety of places and do a variety of things.

Such belief is not without its recompense and even its reward. People confess to finding forgiveness, peace, and a new joy— they reorient themselves and find a kind of justification in God's life and love that they never suspected to be available. More than this they see the world in a new way. Everything is gradually seen to be a gift, given by God himself. No one can begin to see things as gifts unless he is sometimes thankful. So we are urged by the apostle Paul to be thankful in and for all things. And it might well be that learning to be thankful is as much a condition for believing that God created the world (making everything His free gift) as believing in creation is a condition for becoming thankful.

In some such way as this most of the Christian teachings take root in us. And that analogy of "taking root" is no chance remark, for that is how these teachings come to be ours. Most of these teachings grew up in some such fashion as already suggested; for they never did drop down whole and entire from a heavenly source, neither did they spring up from any single human source. They found their expression through the lives of faithful believers. We mistake the import of those teachings if we neglect the lives that nurtured them just as we miss the high points of faith if we neglect the daring beliefs that founded them.

Theological beliefs, then, are strange. The conditions that have to be met before we can claim them are identical with the conditions that were met to make them possible in the first place. Those conditions are not easy, to be sure, but their difficulty is not intellectual either. The theological teachings, what we have called the language of faith, were originally born in the lives of stalwart champions of the Christian life. They came forth from men who suffered, who were hurt by the world, who spent long years in practicing what Jesus asked of them. What they declare about God and the world also bear the signs of birth, for pathos and feeling, passion and earnestness surge through their every line.

Theological beliefs are quite different than scientific and scholarly beliefs. For the originators of science sometimes had to endure hardship and trials too. Some of them tried dozens of experiments and formulated many theories before they met with success. But the ironic fact is that most learning, even the sciences most difficult to master, can be handed down from one generation to the next quite easily. What one learned with the greatest difficulty, another, a student in a modern school, can learn by reading a textbook. Therefore, it is not necessary in our schools and colleges to do much else than teach the results, for, in truth, we can learn the results without the means that produced them in the first place.

But in other matters of the human spirit, it is not quite so. Here the conditions that produced the sayings of faith among the apostles also have to be realized and redone by each of us in turn. Therefore, there is no great progress in theology as there is in science, except on matters of religious thought that is "about" so many things of faith. This progress does not include the language of faith, for here each person must start over with his own life. Each of us must start with the acknowledgment of our guilt just as Paul and the other apostles did, and each of us must do what they did in order to be certain of those things of which they were certain. Here there are no results to be handed down. Those teachings, which are old and which are given us, have to be reclaimed. The way of reclaiming them is everything that makes our consciousness truly Christian—liturgy, hymns, prayers, deeds, the sense of guilt, suffering with Jesus Christ, and thus intending the world.

No wonder, then, that doubting the Christian teaching is so confounding. Our disturbance and our distress is the very stuff, if properly directed, that will perhaps help us to remake our lives.

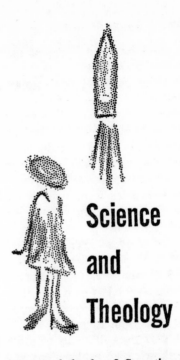

Science
and
Theology

Is there a conflict between science and theology? Sometimes theologians have fought scientists and vice versa. There is little point to denying that fact. In the context of a book on theological matters it is well to admit that often theologians and religious thinkers were as stubborn and as obtuse as the advocates of science were enthusiastic and often unreflective about matters quite alien to their special competencies. The upshot among many students, not least those of us who read those brief historical accounts which preface our science books, is the thought that maybe science has really replaced theological beliefs after all. For sometimes the story is told as if theologians, who believed in old books and venerable churches, opposed new sciences and were simply blind to new methods, evidence, and the need for verification. Sometimes our doubt is fed through such a back way as this, almost as though everything noble once said about the effects of faith and the noble life it describes is made dubious by the memory of the long-standing conflict between science and religion.

Many facets of this conflict have been explored at length quite recently, enough in fact to correct a great number of crude popular views. This is not the place to relate the details of research in intellectual history, but it is an instance where scholarship and knowledge (and language) about religion, and for that matter, also about science and its history, have quite specifically told us that certain views, like that of the conflict between science and religion, previously noted, are false and not worth believing. In short there is no or little justification for holding such views any longer. This is how scholarship sometimes relieves a doubt that was probably planted by poorer scholarship or earlier views.

Unfortunately, the conflict of science with religion is not completely taken care of quite so easily. Whatever one believes about the past, the conflict also tends to rise in the present. For many persons let science and learning simply push religion out of their lives. It looks to some as though one cannot believe both scientific explanations and theological explanations. The theory of evolution looked to Darwin himself as a view which excluded the theological views he had earlier believed. That kind of story could be told by many others, perhaps readers of these pages, who, without being great scientists themselves, find that there is less attachment to their childhood teachings, including their religious teaching, as they mature in the scientific work of others.

We have already spoken of the requirements of doubting in the strictly intellectual disciplines, and we have seen, too, how different our doubts of religious teachings are. From one point of view, religious doubts need a kind of movement of the personality, a shift in one's self-evaluation, in order to be resolved, and cognitive doubts need evidence. This is not all that is to be said, however; there is still another way in which doubts of religious teachings are created and also resolved. As our concluding chapter, we will examine this other and somewhat distinctive source of our conflicts.

2. WAYS OF HANDLING THE WORLD

We have already spoken of our learning to intend the world. Upon inspection it turns out that all of us intend the world in a variety of ways. We handle it, appreciate it, evaluate it, and judge it for a variety of purposes and goals. In such wise, we can say that our consciousness always includes this diversity, and the more gifted we are as persons the greater the variation and the deeper and the more inclusive our conscious ways.

Intending the world with the purpose of explaining its features and finding its order and its laws is very close to being the essence of our intellectual and scientific endeavors. For a great many reasons, knowing the world has all kinds of practical advantages too, and it is often for some of these that we learn our sciences. However that be, modern science has given us great powers and has taught us to believe that everything around us, sooner or later, can be so examined and understood. From small and very crude beginnings, intelligent people have conceived ever-new and important ways to tackle unknown and obscure phenomena. The histories of science and of other kinds of learning, too, are testimony to the success of the race in so doing.

Our interest at this point is not strictly in the growth of the science because that subject is already covered in numerous histories of Western man. Instead, it must be pointed out here that there is a strange consequence of all this, and this consequence is what will engage us. For science, too, causes a change in our temperament, and this is often overlooked. And the difference science makes to us temperamentally frequently causes us to doubt our religion, the esthetic judgments of poets and artists, as well as many common-sense convictions by which we ordinarily live.

Our consciousness, let it be said again, includes a variety of ways of intending the world. The ideal is that our consciousness should be a synthesis, such that no conflicts would arise; but this synthesis is not easy to achieve and to retain. There are several distinctive ways, all of them learned, of intending the world. One is an esthetic and artful way. This seems to depend upon great natural sensitivites and rather rare talents. The language that goes with this is that of the poets and other artistically sensitive people. Their language is the language of the beautiful and the ugly, and this language is both expressive and full of feeling and also about everything and anything in the world. Great esthetic language has power also to make the listener feel the pathos, to sense the beauty, to abhor the ugliness. It also tells us the truth about the world in these terms and in the service of such esthetic capacities as we might possess.

There is more, too; for all of us, perhaps to moderate degree, also respond to and discern the world ethically. Our moral language is another rich and complete testimony to the complexity of both the world and ourselves. Moral language both discerns the nature of the world, discriminating good and evil everywhere, and expresses what a moral man is and wants to be. Learning moral language is one way to become moral just as learning the language of faith is a way to become faithful. However, neither the esthetic language and way of thought nor the moral create such conflicts with religious and Christian ways as does the scientific. In fact, much of religious reflection is already couched in esthetic forms, and ethical language, witness the Old Testament's moral teaching, is often incorporated entire into the Christian's teaching. But science raises another kind of query.

The effect of science is to fashion a very distinctive style of human consciousness. After even brief exposure to the way of intending and handling the world that science is, most students become increasingly questioning and even querulous. The aim in the sciences is to treat everything in a dispassionate and disinterested manner. The conviction soon arises that only in a detached and independent spirit can a man also be impartial and free from prejudice. Therefore, for long centuries, it has been maintained that a strict objectivity of spirit, dispassionate, disinterested, detached, was a necessary condition for knowing the truth about most matters of fact. In brief, this means that the scientific way of intending the world, in its somewhat abstract and impersonal way, is quite different from the esthetic, the moral, and the religious ways.

For in the three latter instances, men are not dispassionate at all. Putting it more concretely, we, ourselves, are not dispassionate except when we do science. Otherwise our lives are a rich mixture of feelings, interests, concerns, loves, and enthusiasms. Therefore, all of us have our poetic moments, our hours of solemn ethical reflection, along with our cognitive and intellectual periods. In justice to the many-sidedness that is ours, we must admit that we count up and evaluate our world in various ways. Nonetheless, our scientific exposure, plus any special training we might have had along the way, suffices to create a very hearty respect for everything associated with the sciences. Consequently, we sometimes lose sight of, and even positively neglect, those other ways of language and all that goes with them.

Scientific and scholarly ways of learning the world are, then, another way to intend the world. This way is not necessarily superior to the others. However, it is better suited to serve the special aims and purposes that we have when we want to know about something or other. Furthermore, the scientific ways are congruent with many tempermental factors which we may have already developed. The result of such a style of consciousness is, of course, what we call knowledge, what we have referred to as an "about" language.

But it is, accordingly, a mistake to assume that theology and science must conflict. In fact, they have in the past and frequently do even now. If what we have argued is at all cogent, theology and science should serve differing uses and differing needs within our consciousness. Then the question is whether a person can keep this diversity of consciousness and the corresponding diversity of languages separated and yet flexible and responsive to differing uses.

Much of the conflict between science and religion stems from the fact that science issues in explanations that are relatively free of interests and concerns, loves and hopes. This is what is meant when we say science is disinterested. On the contrary, Christian theology explains and judges the whole world in the light of the most comprehensive and complete interest a man has, namely, the interest in saving his own life and existence. Therefore, Christian theology tells us how the heavens and the earth, history before and after, everything from the cosmos in the large to the cosmos in the small, work together for the good that matters most. Theology is the most interested of all explanations.

Of course, there is a point to making our reflection absolutely disinterested. All of us know how hard it is to think straight and well if one is prejudiced, predisposed, or so full of feeling that one cannot see the actual facts. Therefore, everyone who is at all intelligent and blessed with a well-developed sense of responsibility must fight to keep scientific inquiry free of being too nationalistic and so designed only to serve interests that are temporary and local. Philosophers who have thought at length about these things have shown us quite clearly that there are ways for you and me to think which will make our thoughts and our language available to all of mankind. This is what we mean by thought which is universal, above parties, nations, and prejudice. In our day, most scientists of all nations work toward such a neutral and nonpartisan kind of knowledge. Objectivity is the guarantee of such universality.

Here we have defended this goal. Nothing said heretofore has been intended to slight in the least the great ideal of modern learning. But the effect upon the individual must also be noted; and here we have remarked upon the fact that the temperamental style—the disinterested and detached observer—is but one component in a well-developed consciousness.

3.   A UNIVERSAL INTEREST

The charge made against human passions and interests, loves and hopes, is frequently that they blind us to the facts and that they engender our prejudices and blind spots, make us partial, and ensure a party mentality. So, a major source of conflict between science and religion grows out of the conviction that all theological reasoning is, because it is passional and interested, also partial and prejudicial. The same is believed about ethical and esthetic judgments too. But theology especially comes in for criticism, and its judgments are often deemed to be churchly, only confessional, belonging to another age, hence old fashioned, biased, and unduly influenced by factors that ought not to count.

The outcome is plain enough to see. Young persons, schooled in our science-saturated curricula and society, often develop the dark suspicion that the theological teachings of their churches are really not quite proper. Most of theology, because it is not subject to the same rules of evidence and techniques of justification, begins to fit the description of prejudicial views we have noted above. Often the doubts that develop rest upon a suspicion that gets stronger and stronger the longer and more thorough our scientific practice. Because we are not clear about how these teachings do fit with our sciences, our skepticism of religious teachings remains terribly alive.

In previous pages, some helpful distinctions were drawn. It must be remembered, it was said, that there are two kinds of doubt and two kinds of justification. Science handles one kind and one kind only; and religion (the whole enterprise, liturgy, worship, stories, and theology) handles the other. We went further and said there were two kinds of religious thought, one "about" the religion, which was cognitive and scientific, the other "of" the religion, which was cognitive all right but was also an expression of a different way of intending the world than was common to the sciences.

Now, however, one more issue must be met. Because theology expresses an interest, because it is passional, is it therefore only a prejudice? Is there no truth in it? Is it only a point of view?

We can grant the need for protection against the passions. Any one of us can testify to this. A mother is seldom the best person to give a completely candid and detailed analysis of her daughter's life, for she is too close to the subject and cares too much. A soldier, who has been often in battle, is seldom the one to give a disinterested account of the enemies' cultural strengths. But does this say that all interests and concerns are equally disturbing and distorting to a candid and true judgment?

The Christian's account ought to give one pause. For Christianity insists that not all interests are the same. Not every interest is whimsical, chancy, and an accident of time, birth, and fortune. Certainly, some interests are like that. Some nations eat potatoes, others feed them to animals; therefore, the enthusiasm for potatoes is an impossible one to use to judge all mankind. So, too, with preference for wine over water, blondes over brunettes, and hundreds of other interests and concerns. Now that we know so much about cultures and societies other than our own, we also know dangers of using cultural preferences of one people to judge others. Modern social sciences are increasingly trying to explain social phenomena without using cultural preferences and practices.

Indeed we know, then, how important it is to be certain that our sciences, especially about people, are disinterested and even culture-free. But still, the point of Christian theology is that there is at least one interest and concern that is not simply a cultural matter, not a preference, and not a localism of time or place. This is the interest in one's own justification. Christianity builds its entire appeal and case upon an interest that is universal and is necessary. Hence, this interest in being justified and approved, in being found worthy, is not simply a first-century A.D. matter, not a cultic phenomenon, not a matter for either Jews or Gentiles, but is finally an interest of all men.

This interest is, therefore, a bond between past and present, Jesus and you, Gentile and Jew, and it makes brothers of all nations and tribes. This is why the early Christians had to work so hard to understand the Gospel story in terms that were not Jewish alone, for there was a temptation on the part of the earliest Christians, who had been Jews, to make Christianity a little more culturally Jewish than it really was. So, too, later Christians made theology and liturgy seem so Latin that it lost some of its universal appeal. The European Reformers, not least Luther and his followers, almost succeeded in making the theology Germanic and again somewhat parochial. Against these malformations, theologians must always work to make the Christian message truly universal.

Therefore, the overarching concern of Christian teachers has been to address all men, regardless of their heritage, race, color, nation, and disposition. Theology and the practices of the churches are aimed primarily at the human condition. To the extent that they succeed, men become conscious of their own state and acknowledge their condition. The most elemental consequent of Christian nurture is, therefore, the most candid self-appraisal, that which we referred to earlier as a kind of self-doubt or despair. And Jesus of Nazareth and the teachings associated with His name are directed to such people. They begin to count meaningfully only to such people.

It is not just, therefore, to criticize every theological teaching on the grounds that it is a statement of interest. The question that matters is whether the interest is trivial or great, optional or necessary, local or universal? Interests which are universal and necessary, which are finally inescapable, are not deceptive. The fact is that once we understand that our interest and the interest of all men is being served, then we can also understand that God died for all of us and that the entire drama of salvation is on our behalf. Under such circumstances, understanding flourishes and there is born a new community of men, wedded in a common debt to a common Savior, who is Christ, the Lord.

4. DOUBT THAT SERVES

Doubts may come and go. Most serious religious doubts are directed against, as we have insisted all along, Christian theology. But what is Christian theology? Is it the prejudice of a class? of the priests and parties? an invention of the first century? We have given all that we could to the air of doubt and skepticism. We have said that it was necessary to gaining intellectual maturity. Furthermore, doubt is useful simply to free us from the trivializing array of temporary fancies and whimsical asides that continually come our way.

This is why we can say that there is a kind of doubt that is of positive service to a Christian consciousness. For Christianity teaches us that if we will utterly lose our life and fail miserably it will be because of our interests. Our interests, our enthusiasms, and our passions will either lead us astray or they will lead us to a saved and meaningful life. Unlike some kind of austere ways of life which say, like the ancient stories, that men ought to be apathetic, that is, without pathos, interests, and feelings, Christianity proposes to educate our feelings and interests. The doubt which is of service to faith is, thus, the doubt directed against our passions, loves, and interests. Most of them produce headlong and enthusiastic behavior, most of which we come later to regret. Christian nurture tends to give us pause here and criticizes severely our passional patterns. Christian nurture brings our sexual passions into marriage, and loving then becomes a task of a lifetime, not a weekend episode. So, too, does Christian nurture cast doubt upon the wisdom of our youthful whims, our overpowering desire for cars, for money, for immediate successes, by teaching that when all these things pass away, when even knowledge fails, the love of God, which is deep and inclusive, pure and wise, will never pass away.

The story of the world is the story of God's love, mostly frustrated but sometimes completely victorious. Christian theology is that account and must be so understood. But its aim is not simply to inform you and certainly not to amuse you. The aim of theology is to help you correct your own interests and win your own life and reward. The seat of the difficulties, it asserts, is you! Here is where all these things come together. We began, pages ago, describing the kinds of doubt. The kind we called religious leads a person to doubt the validity of his present life, especially the constellation of interests and concerns that give him his goals and purposes. It is the task of theology to make him happy in the realization that, after all, he is also the child of God and that a new and fully justifiable life is open to him.

The best part of the story is, of course, that all of this is the gift of God to each. Perhaps if this story has been well told, each reader will admit that only a fool will refuse such a gift.